Contents

AS November gets closer and the Biden administration gets more murderous and tyrannical by the day, liberal spinmeisters are falling all over themselves to portray the president as some kind of passive witness to the atrocities we're witnessing in Gaza and the authoritarian suppression of dissent we're seeing in the US. No no, he's completely powerless to stop the government that's completely dependent on US military support from conducting a military operation. No no, he's completely powerless to stop the violent police crackdowns he's openly supporting and encouraging on protesters against his genocide.

Bullshit. Biden has always been a murderous swamp monster. That's the only reason he got the job. And that's why the cover of today's issue of JOHNSTONE features the US president dining on an ice cream cone of gore.

All works are written by Caitlin Johnstone and Tim Foley. The Caitlin Johnstone project is 100 percent reader-funded.

Visit caitlinjohnst.one for the original articles and their supporting links.

Biden Wanted To Sanction An Israeli Battalion But He Didn't Because Israel Said No

The Biden administration has reportedly canned its plans to issue sanctions on an extremist IDF unit for human rights violations in the occupied West Bank, following backlash from Israel and its high-powered supporters within the US government.

Axios reports:

> The State Department has put on hold its intention to impose sanctions on the Israel Defense Forces "Netzah Yehuda" battalion for human rights violations in the occupied West Bank and is reviewing the issue in light of information Israel provided in recent days, U.S. sources familiar with the issue said.

> Why it matters: The review is part of a consultation process outlined in an agreement between the U.S. and Israel. But Secretary of State Antony Blinken has also been under extensive pressure from the Israeli government, members of Congress and some senior Biden administration officials to reconsider the possible sanctions.

The big picture: The Biden administration had intended to withhold U.S. military aid and training from the Netzah Yehuda battalion—an unprecedented move in the history of relations between the countries.

As Dr Assal Rad has highlighted on Twitter, this decision follows a sequence of events in which ProPublica revealed that Secretary of State Antony Blinken was ignoring his own State Department's recommendation to sanction Israeli military units that have been credibly accused of human rights abuses like rape and torture, after which Blinken announced that he was preparing to issue sanctions after all. This announcement was met with outrage from Israel and its apologists, with Israeli Prime Minister Benjamin Netanyahu penning a furious screed calling the planned sanctions "the height of absurdity and a moral low". Those planned sanctions are now canceled.

Or to put it more simply, the Biden administration had planned to sanction an IDF battalion, but it didn't because Israel said no.

Which would be about par for the White House under Joseph R Biden, who throughout his too-long political career has received more campaign funding from the Israel lobby than literally anyone else in Washington. As Quincy Institute's Trita Parsi recently explained in an article for Foreign Policy, this administration's adamant refusal to set any limits whatsoever with the Israeli state is a dramatic deviation from the norm, with other presidents frequently displaying a well-documented willingness to give Tel Aviv a smack whenever it got too insane.

This incident with the IDF battalion sanctions is a good example of the way the Biden administration has had a standing policy of pretty much just letting Israel write its own rules for itself in Washington. We saw this illustrated yet again in a recent exchange at a press briefing with Deputy State Department Spokesman Vedant Patel, who when asked about the mass graves being discovered in Gaza kept defending the administration's line that this was something Israel needs to investigate for itself.

Here's a transcript:

PATEL: Go ahead, with the glasses.

QUESTION: Thank you.

QUESTION: The Gaza civil service today held a press conference this morning, which was televised, and they said that evidence showed that many of those pulled out from the three mass graves that they found, including children, were tortured before being killed. Some even showed signs of being buried alive, along with other crimes against humanity that they accused Israeli forces of. They called for an independent forensic investigation. This administration repeatedly says that it asked Israel—the Israeli Government—to investigate itself.

As a mediator for peace between Israelis and Palestinians, how does it ever make sense that the United States asked the accused party to examine itself and provide reports that you have previously said that you actually trust? What's wrong with an independent, scientific, forensic investigation? I mean, if there—if the results of such an independent investigation prove the accusations to be baseless, then that would be in Israel's favor, wouldn't it?

PATEL: So as it relates to the continued reporting about—we're seeing about these mass graves, first, National Security Advisor

Assal Rad
@AssalRad · Follow

-Story gets out that Blinken is ignoring Israeli human rights abuses
-PR story appears that Biden admin is going to do something
-Israel publicly acts outraged that laws may apply to them
-Biden admin quietly decides to do nothing

What a perfect summary of this admin

ProPublica: Blinken Ignored His Agency's Recommendation to Disqualify Some Israeli Units from Aid
HEADLINE APR 16, 2024

Scoop: U.S. expected to sanction IDF unit for human rights violations in West Bank

Netanyahu's Outraged Response After Report of Pending US Sanctions on IDF
Published Apr 20, 2024 at 7:53 PM EDT

U.S. won't sanction IDF units over 'gross human rights violations' - report
Biden administration determined that the IDF units in question, including the Netzah Yehuda battalion, committed human rights violations against Palestinians in the West Bank

2:27 AM · Apr 27, 2024

8.3K   Reply   Copy link

Read 106 replies

Sullivan spoke a little bit about this yesterday, but we continue to find these reports incredibly troubling. And that's why yesterday you saw the National Security Advisor call for this to be thoroughly investigated. We want to see these facts looked into. And simultaneously, we're continuing to press the Government of Israel for more information. The IDF has spoken to this in some sense already, but we are continuing to press them for additional information.

QUESTION: But why not have an independent, forensic scientific—which the Palestinians are calling for?

PATEL: We think this does need to be thoroughly investigated, but in terms of the modality, we continue to want to see some additional information from the Government of Israel before we make other assessments.

QUESTION: But you're asking the accused to investigate itself.

PATEL: We believe that through a thorough investigation, we can get some additional answers. We're also hoping to continue to get more information from the Government of Israel on this.

QUESTION: But to his—

PATEL: Guita, go ahead.

Assal Rad
@AssalRad · Follow

Reporter: Evidence at Gaza mass graves show torture and signs of being buried alive, Palestinians called for an independent investigation, what's wrong with that?

Patel: We're asking Israel

Reporter: You're asking the accused to investigate itself?

Patel: We're asking Israel

3:51 AM · Apr 26, 2024

Have you ever seen anything more absurd?

Having a position that literally every accusation of Israeli criminality in Gaza just means Israel needs to investigate itself is exactly the same as having a position that Israel can commit any crime it wants with no consequences whatsoever, because obviously Israel is never going to convict itself of any wrongdoing. But that is indeed the Biden administration's position.

The message that Israel has been consistently getting from Washington from October 7 onward is, do whatever you like. Commit whatever crimes you want to commit. Our support is unconditional and there will be no consequences for any of your actions, ever. And Israel is certainly taking up every bit of slack it's being given on that front.

Featured image via U.S. Embassy Jerusalem (CC BY 2.0 DEED)

$95.3B IN AID TO ISRAEL, UKRAINE & TAIWAN
U.S. SENATE — SEN. PETE RICKETTS R–Nebraska — C·SPAN 45 YEARS
Today

Empire Managers Say Russia, China And Iran Are Tricking Students Into Opposing Genocide

Empire managers and propagandists are losing their minds about student protests against the genocide in Gaza on university campuses, so naturally we're seeing a mad push to frame this as the result of interference by Russia, China, Iran and Hamas. These demented conspiracies of foreign influence come even as Israel's prime minister openly calls for the US government to quash the university protests by any means necessary.

In a speech supporting the ban of TikTok this past Tuesday, Senator Pete Ricketts said the protests are an example of "the Chinese Communist Party using TikTok to skew public opinion on foreign events."

"Look what's happening in our college campuses right now around this country," Ricketts said. "Pro-Hamas activists are taking over public spaces and making it impossible for campuses to operate."

"Why is this happening?" Ricketts continued. "Well, let's look at where young people are getting their news. Nearly a third of adults 18 to 29, these young people in the US are regularly getting their news exclusively from TikTok. Pro-Palestinian and pro-Hamas hashtags are generating 50 times the views on TikTok right now despite the fact that polling shows Americans overwhelmingly support Israel over Hamas. These videos have more reach than the top 10 news websites combined. This is not coincidence. The Chinese Communist Party is doing this on purpose. They are pushing this racist agenda with the intention of undermining our democratic values. And if you look at what's happening at Columbia University and other campuses across the country right now, they're winning."

These comments from Ricketts are repugnant and deceitful in a whole host of ways, but let's touch on the big ones.

The senator's claim that TikTok is being manipulated to artificially amplify pro-Palestine content is false, as evidenced

Michael Tracey ✓
@mtracey · Follow

X

Sen. Pete Ricketts (R-NE) comes right out and admits it: they're about to ban TikTok because "young people are getting their news" from the app, and "pro-Palestinian" hashtags generate lots of views. He says Chinese Communists are "pushing this racist agenda" to undermine America

> Watch on X
> $95.3B IN AID TO ISRAEL, UKRAINE & TAIWAN
> U.S. SENATE
> SEN. PETE RICKETTS
> @SenatorRicketts
> C·SPAN2

9:51 AM · Apr 24, 2024

♡ 3.7K   Reply   Copy link

by the fact that TikTok's US-based rivals Facebook and Instagram have been showing the same massive gaps between the popularity of pro-Palestine content and the popularity of pro-Israel content. His argument is as logically fallacious as claiming that flat earth content is being artificially suppressed because it's not as popular as round earth content. Pro-Israel content is just less popular, because it sucks and people don't like it.

Ricketts' assertion that "polling shows Americans overwhelmingly support Israel over Hamas" is deceitful; polling shows a majority of Americans oppose Israel's actions in Gaza, regardless of whether they "support" the Palestinian militant group Hamas.

Also noteworthy is the way Ricketts just comes right out and acknowledges that TikTok is presenting a problem because its pro-Palestine content has been going viral among young people in ways the legacy media can't compete with. This amounts to an admission that empire managers like Pete Ricketts really just want TikTok to be banned because young people are using it to share unauthorized ideas and information with each other, and

The Recount ✓
@therecount · Follow

X

Former House Speaker Nancy Pelosi suggests some pro-Palestinian protests, especially those against President Biden, have "a Russian tinge to it."

"It's in Putin's interest for 'What's His Name' to win, and therefore I see some encouragement on the part of the Russians."

> Watch on X
> RTÉ News

3:27 AM · Apr 25, 2024

♡ 673   Reply   Copy link

would support its elimination even if they couldn't justify it under the pretense of fighting China.

It's probably also worth noting that Rickets has received at least $159,000 from the Israel lobby.

Former House Speaker Nancy Pelosi repeated the fartbrained opinion she's been voicing for months that anti-genocide demonstrations can be attributed to Russia, telling RTÉ News this past Wednesday that opposition to President Biden's backing of an active genocide has "a Russian tinge to it".

"It's in Putin's interest for 'What's His Name' to win, and therefore I see some encouragement on the part of the Russians," said the longtime Democratic Party leader in reference to Donald Trump.

Anti-Defamation League president Jonathan Greenblatt says it's actually Iran who's tricking all these university students into thinking genocide is bad, telling MSNBC that the two main organizations behind the demonstrations—the Students for Justice in Palestine and Jewish Voice for Peace—are actually "campus proxies" of Iran.

"Iran has their military proxies like Hezbollah, and Iran has their campus proxies like these groups like SJP and JVP," Greenblatt proclaimed on literally no basis whatsoever.

The Wall Street Journal tells us that rather than China, Russia or Iran, it's actually Hamas, Hezbollah and the Houthis who are behind the university campus protests.

In an article titled "Who's Behind the Anti-Israel Protests," subtitled "Hamas, Hezbollah, the Houthis and others are grooming activists in the U.S. and across the West," The Wall Street Journal's Steven Stalinsky makes another one of his signature chowderheaded arguments based entirely on vague insinuations, shoulder-socket-jeopardizing reach, Gish gallop fallacy, and no real evidence of any kind.

"Six months after the attack on Israel, Hamas, Hezbollah, the Houthis and others aren't merely cheering those protesting in the streets," writes Stalinsky. "They are working with and grooming activists in the U.S. and the West, through meetings, online interviews and podcasts."

No no, not meetings, online interviews and podcasts! No wonder they were able to hypnotize university students into opposing daily massacres against a walled-in population driven by ethnically motivated hatred.

'WHAT'S HAPPENING ON AMERICA'S COLLEGE CAMPUSES IS HORRIFIC'

Stalinsky runs a think tank called the Middle East Media Research Institute (MEMRI), which was literally founded by a former Israeli intelligence officer. Pro-Palestine activist and academic Norman Finkelstein has accused MEMRI of using "the same sort of propaganda techniques as the Nazis," and even brazenly unprincipled empire propagandist Brian Whitaker has written that MEMRI "poses as a research institute when it's basically a propaganda operation."

All this drooling imbecility about completely fictional foreign interference being responsible for these campus protests looks even more ridiculous as the Israeli prime minister unabashedly flexes his nation's extensive influence over US politics to call for a crackdown on campus demonstrations.

"What's happening in America's college campuses is horrific. Antisemitic mobs have taken over leading universities," Benjamin Netanyahu said in a statement, addressing the American public in his perfect American English.

"It has to be stopped," Netanyahu continued. "It has to be condemned and condemned unequivocally. But that's not what happened. The response of several university presidents was shameful. Now, fortunately, state, local, federal officials, many of them have responded differently but there has to be more. More has to be done."

It is a very dark kind of hilarious to see imperial spinmeisters falling all over themselves trying to spin the campus protests as a product of imaginary foreign interference even as police launch violent crackdowns on those very same protesters across the United States to advance the interests of a foreign government.

It's also a big loogie in the eye of any self-respecting free thinker. Unless your brain has been turned into bean curd by empire propaganda, the idea that young people would need to be manipulated into opposing the incomprehensible horrors that are being inflicted upon human beings in Gaza is an appalling insult to your intelligence.

But that just shows how desperate these freaks are getting. More and more people are waking up from the lies they've been fed about their government, their nation and their world as western institution after western institution completely discredits itself in the eyes of the mainstream public trying to defend the most indefensible things imaginable.

They're frantically scrambling to try to remedy this PR crisis they've created for themselves, but everything they've tried so far has been a pathetic failure that has only made things worse for them, turning an entire generation into wide awake radicals whose bright young eyes will never, ever unsee what they have seen.

Feature image is a screenshot from C-SPAN

Quashing University Protests And Banning TikTok To Make The Kids Love Israel
• Notes From The Edge Of The Narrative Matrix •

It's just a tough situation, with victims on both sides. On one side you've got people being slaughtered in droves by genocidal massacres and siege warfare, while on the other you've got people whose feelings get hurt when these atrocities are opposed. Hard to say which is worse.

•

Assal Rad
@AssalRad · Follow

𝕏

This video is unbelievable.

Students and teachers are being arrested for protesting US support for atrocities in Gaza. Now reporters are getting assaulted and arrested for covering the protests. But remember, democracy is on the ballot.

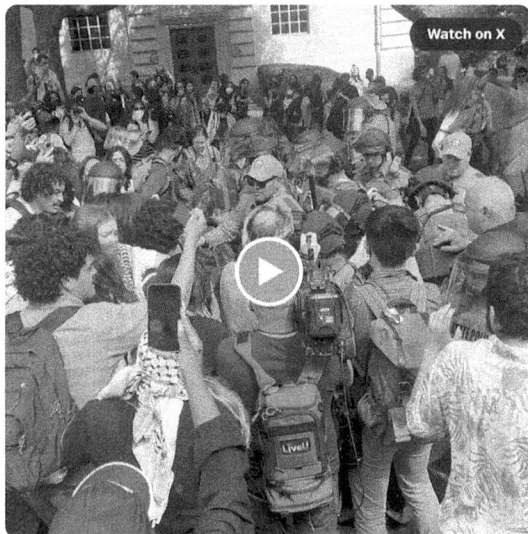

Watch on X

9:41 AM · Apr 25, 2024

ⓘ

♥ 11.8K   💬 Reply   ⤴ Copy link

Read 568 replies

I have dedicated every day of my life to the project of spreading awareness of the depravity and deceitfulness of the western empire, but I will never write anything more effective toward this end than what the empire is doing itself on university campuses right now.

I mean, you kind of have to wonder what they're thinking. "Yeah, that's it. Violently quash pro-Palestine protests at universities, ban TikTok to ensure the suppression of pro-Palestine content, and saturate the boomer media with obvious propaganda. That'll make the kids love Israel."

•

Meanwhile the US empire is still playing games with each and every one of our lives by continually taking insane risks in its world-threatening brinkmanship with a nuclear superpower. It turns out last month the Biden administration secretly sent Ukraine long-range Army Tactical Missile Systems (ATACMS), which Ukraine has reportedly already used to attack a Russian base in Crimea.

In 2022 when Ukraine first started urging the United States to send it the ATACMS— which has nearly four times the range of the HIMARS weapons the US has been supplying—Russia's Foreign Ministry spokeswoman Maria Zakharova immediately responded with a warning that their use on Russian territory would make the US a direct participant in the conflict, and Russia would respond accordingly. Crimea is considered Russian territory by the Russian Federation.

In an article published in Antiwar last year titled "ATACMS: Be Very Afraid of This Acronym," West Suburban Peace Coalition president Walt Zlotow wrote that this missile system "has potential to draw the US and NATO into all out war with Russia":

ATACMS are long range US missiles that can strike up to 190 miles. Top US officials, likely including President Biden, are seriously considering giving ATACMS to Ukraine in their battle to take back all Russian gains in Ukraine, including Crimea. They can reach both Crimea and the Russian mainland.

If so used by Ukraine to attack Russia, it may be a missile too far that could ignite Russian tactical nuclear weapons in Ukraine. Further escalation into nuclear confrontation between Russia and the US/NATO alliance seeking Russia's defeat becomes more likely.

•

Biden proclaimed it "a good day for world peace" when he signed the World War 3 bill which will pour weapons of death and destruction into Israel, Ukraine and Taiwan. This is the inverted reality the US-centralized empire premises its narratives about itself upon. They've got the mainstream public espousing a completely backwards and upside-down worldview, which is why we live in a completely backwards and upside-down civilization.

•

The Ukraine war funding part of the bill was actually reportedly pushed through with behind-the-scenes collaboration between Trump and Republican lawmakers. Anyone who still buys Trump's "ending the wars, fighting the deep state" schtick is a fucking moron.

Michael Tracey @mtracey · Follow

Biden just signed the mammoth war funding bill. "It's a good day for world peace," he says, without a hint of irony. New arms shipments will flow to Ukraine within hours. It's a shame Trump couldn't be there for the signing ceremony, they could've bonded over their shared support

1:42 AM · Apr 25, 2024

635   Reply   Copy link

Read 81 replies

•   •

When Israel's genocide funding made it through the House, Benjamin Netanyahu tweeted, "The US Congress just overwhelmingly passed a much appreciated aid bill that demonstrates strong bipartisan support for Israel and defends Western civilization. Thank you friends, thank you America!"

And he's not wrong. The US congress does have massive bipartisan support for Israel, and pouring war machinery into that genocidal apartheid state does in fact bolster the blood-fueled machine of nonstop murder and tyranny that is "western civilization".

Human thriving arises from curiosity. Curiosity about the way our material universe operates leads to advances in science, and all the benefits that come with it. Curiosity about how our civilization's power structures operate leads to an understanding of how the world really works, which will lead to the emergence of a truth-based society if realized on a collective level. Curiosity about our own consciousness and inner processes leads to self-realization, and the harmonious way of moving in the world which flows from it.

If a healthy humanity exists in the future, it will be above all a deeply curious species. The values of competition, greed and domination which currently drive the way our civilization operates will have given way to curiosity, humility and discovery. We will have cultivated a humble but intense curiosity about ourselves, about each other, about our collective societal dynamics, and about our natural world.

Featured images via Rawpixel, Wannapic, Freepic, and Wikimedia Commons.

Palestinians being massacred

Western Zionists feeling offended

Israel Is Turning Hospitals Into Mass Graves While The West Fixates On 'Antisemitism'

A mass grave created by the IDF has been uncovered at a Gaza hospital, where Palestinian civilians appear to have been the victims of a gruesome massacre.

"Bah, that's old news Caitlin," you may be saying. "We already know about the massacre and mass graves which were discovered a few weeks ago at the al-Shifa Hospital in Gaza."

No no, that's a different mass grave from a different IDF massacre at a completely different Gaza hospital. The now completely destroyed al-Shifa Hospital was in Gaza City; I'm talking about the Nasser Medical Complex in Khan Younis, where some 210 bodies have reportedly been discovered in a mass grave after Israeli forces withdrew from the city earlier this month. Two different massacres, two different hospitals, two different mass graves full of Palestinian civilians.

The IDF are just attacking hospitals and mowing down civilians and trying to bury the evidence of their crimes, so naturally we're seeing the western political-media class focus very hard on the problem of antisemitism allegations on college campuses.

"Biden denounces antisemitism on college campuses amid Columbia protests," reads a new headline from The Washington Post.

"As Protests Continue at Columbia, Some Jewish Students Feel Targeted," The New York Times urgently warns us.

"White House condemns 'blatantly antisemitic' protests as agitators engulf Columbia University," blares Fox News.

"Columbia University faces full-blown crisis as rabbi calls for Jewish students to 'return home'," says CNN.

Motasem A Dalloul
@AbujomaaGaza · Follow

MoH: Number of bodies retrieved from Nasser Hospital in Khan Younis rises to 210.

Hundreds are still missing!

First picture from Nasser and the second from Al Shifa Hospital!

7:01 PM · Apr 22, 2024

"Columbia University: White House condemns antisemitism at college protests," the BBC reports.

Getting far less attention than the fact that some Zionist university students are feeling uncomfortable feelings because other students say Palestinians are human beings is the fact that Israel is establishing a pattern of massacring civilians and burying them in mass graves outside hospitals in Gaza, or the fact that the IDF has been butchering children in Rafah, or the fact that the International Criminal Court is reportedly considering charging Benjamin Netanyahu and other Israeli officials for war crimes.

Zachary Foster ✔
@_ZachFoster · Follow

How did we get a point where people are more worried that Jewish students at Columbia feel uncomfortable by chants to end Israel's genocide in Gaza than they are worried about the safety of the people facing a genocide?

Absolutely unreal.

6:08 AM · Apr 22, 2024

Motasem A Dalloul
@AbujomaaGaza · Follow

MoH: Number of bodies retrieved from Nasser Hospital in Khan Younis rises to 210.

Hundreds are still missing!

First picture from Nasser and the second from Al Shifa Hospital!

7:01 PM · Apr 22, 2024

630   Reply   Copy link

Read 17 replies

Those matters are important, just not nearly as important as how some western Jews feel emotionally upset about pro-Palestine protests. For that, the world must stop spinning on its axis until this extremely egregious problem has been addressed.

All the western spin and distortion around Israel's mass atrocities in Gaza these last six months have revolved around centering feelings over human lives. How western Jewish Zionists are feeling about pro-Palestine sentiments. How Joe Biden's feelings secretly feel about Netanyahu. How Israelis feel about October 7.

Wherever there's an opportunity to focus the narrative on what feelings are being felt by a politically convenient population, the western press fall all over themselves to do so with tumescent enthusiasm. Wherever there's an opportunity to focus on Israeli atrocities, the western press are nowhere to be found.

If you belong to a group that isn't supported by the western empire, you can see your entire family murdered right in front of you and the western political-media class still won't consider you a victim. If you belong to a group that the empire regards as human, then even someone offending your feelings will be viewed as an unforgivable hate crime.

•

In This Dystopia, Opposing A Genocide Is Considered Worse Than Committing One

All the frenzied shrieking about pro-Palestine protests at universities these last few days makes it clear that our civilization is so twisted and insane that it sees protesting a genocide as far worse than committing one. Which is about as backwards as any society could possibly be.

Briahna Joy Gray ✓
@briebriejoy · Follow

X

I had to scroll past *four* college campus stories, including two protest-critical opeds (John McWhorter & Bret Stephens) before I got to the much delayed coverage of hundreds of Palestinians found in mass graves.

Brandon @bigtylr

I read the NYT article about the mass graves. Filled with really haunting details. Bodies handcuffed and shot. Digging bodies up and then reburying them in a mass grave "with respect" and the eerie silence from the army when asked to confirm if they shot people who were fleeing.

10:57 AM · Apr 24, 2024

2.4K   Reply   Copy link

Read 41 replies

Seriously, try to imagine a crazier, more upside-down civilization than one which gets more angry at people protesting genocidal atrocities than it does at people committing them. A civilization where people wear their pants on their head and walk backwards all day? That would be less crazy. A civilization where the dogs own the people and the children go to work while the parents go to school? That would be less crazy.

It's as wrong as you can possibly get anything in this world. It's actually hard to imagine how anyone could get anything more wrong. If you've accepted daily massacres of innocent civilians as the baseline normal and appropriate thing, and regard any opposition to this as a freakish and evil abomination, then you're as screwed up and confused about reality as any other stark raving lunatic in town. Maybe worse.

To view nonstop mass military slaughter as moral and opposition thereto as immoral is to live in a mental moral universe that has been flipped on its head. It's to inhabit a reality tunnel that has become completely divorced from reality. But that's the kind of mainstream worldview that the political-media class in this society are working to indoctrinate us into day in and day out throughout our entire lives.

I just saw a tweet from the commentator Briahna Joy Gray saying that in order to find any mention in The New York Times of the hundreds of Palestinians in mass graves that are being discovered in Gaza, she had to scroll past no fewer than four stories about pro-Palestine protests on college campuses—including two op-eds which criticized the protesters. ·

What kind of warped, fucked up dystopia is this where that's the kind of mainstream news outlet people are getting their information and ideas from? Our entire civilization is saturated with reality-distorting propaganda like this, and it's making people insane. It's got our moral compasses flipped 180 degrees from our true north, and our inner sensemaker tuning in to frequencies of nothing but garbled static.

That's how crazy they need us to be to keep us supporting a globe-spanning empire that literally cannot exist without nonstop violence and tyranny. They need us thinking up is down and black is white. They need us not just unable to tell the difference between right and wrong, but actually believing that wrong is right and right is wrong. So they pound our collective consciousness day in and day out with extremely aggressive psyops in the form of mass media propaganda to ensure that our insides are scrambled around enough to consent to the amount of depravity necessary for our rulers to continue dominating this planet.

This is what our ruling class has decided will be normal, as Aaron Bushnell said moments before lighting himself on fire in protest of the genocide in Gaza. A society where mass graves get less media attention than university protesters. A society where more political firepower is going into stopping pro-Palestine demonstrations on college campuses than ending Israel's murderous assault on an enclosed enclave packed full of children. A society where trying to stop a genocide is considered evil, and committing one is considered good.

Featured image via Adobe Stock.

Stopping The Slaughter In Gaza Is More Important Than Your Feelings

Stopping the slaughter in Gaza is more important than your feelings. Your feelings don't matter.

Stopping the slaughter in Gaza is more important than playing along with the persecution-LARPing of Zionist university students.

Stopping the slaughter in Gaza is more important than some privileged Ivy Leaguers pretending to feel "unsafe" or "unwelcome" on campus.

Stopping the slaughter in Gaza is more important than whatever you're pretending to believe "From the river to the sea, Palestine will be free" means.

Stopping the slaughter in Gaza is more important than making sure everyone says all the right words and condemns Hamas with sufficient fervor.

Stopping the slaughter in Gaza is more important than making sure Joe Biden maintains enough support to win re-election.

Stopping the slaughter in Gaza is more important than performing all kinds of mental contortions and prostrations while talking about Israel's criminality to avoid offending people who make everything about themselves.

Stopping the slaughter in Gaza is more important than helping you avoid the uncomfortable cognitive dissonance incurred by the contradictions between your stated value system and the genocidal murderousness and cruelty of apartheid Israel.

Your feelings are not more important than Palestinian lives.

Your feelings are not more important than Palestinian displacement.

Your feelings are not even more important than Palestinian feelings.

Your feelings are not important. Stopping the ethnic cleansing and genocide of the people of Gaza is important.

It is a symptom of the cancerousness of western civilization that there are people living their whole lives under the entirely unquestioned assumption that their feelings are so important that it is fine and normal to expect that a limitless number of impoverished foreigners may be killed without any opposition whatsoever in order to promote the interests of their favorite ethnostate, and that anyone who does oppose it is persecuting them.

It is a symptom of how diseased our entire society has become that people are so narcissistic that they now perceive anti-genocide demonstrations on university campuses as a direct attack against them and their identity, and will use any amount of spin and mental contortion to make this seem true.

It is a symptom of the dire need to dismantle the entire western empire that a mainstream narrative structure exists in our society which says opposing a genocide is a far more egregious offense than committing one.

It is a symptom of the dire need for radical revolutionary changes in this civilization that western political systems are urgently discussing the need to stomp out protests against a genocide at university campuses under the pretense of protecting people's feelings.

Don't protect people's feelings. Stop the genocide in Gaza.

People's feelings should be uncomfortable when a genocide is happening.

People should be experiencing uncomfortable cognitive dissonance and shame when their innately unjust worldview is being completely discredited in front of everyone.

None of us should be feeling comfortable with any of this. We should be feeling very, very uncomfortable, and letting that discomfort drive us to end this nightmare forever.

Feature image via Ted Eytan (CC BY-SA 4.0 DEED)

In Gaza The Sniper Drones Are Crying Like Babies

They're hunting civilians with armed quadcopters in Gaza.

The drones play recordings of crying babies and women screaming in distress in order to lure people out into the open, and then shoot them.

This is reportedly happening at the Nuseirat refugee camp in central Gaza, where people live in total darkness at night and have no connection to the outside world.

Other times the drones play the sounds of explosions and gunshots and rolling tanks, and sometimes songs in Hebrew or Arabic, all to terrorize these refugees hiding in the darkness afraid for their lives.

This is the sort of report that a critical thinker would normally dismiss as absurd atrocity propaganda if it was being made about any other military power, but this is the IDF we're talking about, and this specific allegation is pretty well-supported now.

When the destruction of Gaza first began I used to read the jarring claims about the horrific things the IDF were doing and often think, "No, no way. That can't be the whole story. It's too cartoonishly evil. There must be some information missing." Then a few days or weeks later confirmation would come out, showing it's even worse than I thought before.

I don't experience that kind of dubiousness when reading such stories anymore. There are only so many atrocities you can see documented, so many videos of IDF troops recording themselves gleefully behaving like monsters, so many hospitals you can see attacked, so many journalists you can see assassinated, before you read a new report about new unfathomable acts of depravity and find yourself saying "Yeah, that sounds about right."

This baby-crying-sniper-drone story is something else, though. It's like something out of a weird post-apocalyptic horror movie or something. It's the kind of information that makes you sort of re-evaluate your previous assumptions about humanity, the world, and the kind of reality we're experiencing here.

It is really astonishing, how cruel people can be. How cruel a whole nation of people can be made to be, if they're indoctrinated just right. You spend your whole childhood being indoctrinated into the belief that one group of people are inferior to your own and don't deserve the same rights and treatment your group receives, and before you know it you're blockading aid trucks from bringing that group food, and playing recordings of crying babies on an assassination drone in order to murder civilians at a refugee camp.

That's how Nazi Germany happened, it's how the genocidal apartheid state of Israel has happened, and it's how the murderous US-centralized empire has happened. It turns out it's not all that hard to manipulate a population into supporting shocking abuses at mass scale with modern propaganda and indoctrination from early childhood. It turns out the human mind is a lot more hackable than we'd like to believe it is, and that this can be used to unleash living nightmares upon our world a lot more easily than we're comfortable acknowledging.

This is how the entire western world has been manipulated into accepting nonstop war, militarism, nuclear brinkmanship, imperialism and exploitation as fine and normal, and into assuming that a better world isn't possible. As long as the powerful are able to manipulate the way a sufficiently large percentage of the population thinks, speaks, acts and votes, we're going to be stuck in this horrifying dystopia where the sky rains fire upon the innocent, where war profiteers reap vast fortunes from machines which rip apart human bodies, and where sniper drones cry like babies.

We can help weaken the empire's propaganda machine by spreading awareness of what it's doing and how it operates, because propaganda only works if you don't know it's happening to you. Help people to see the ways in which the mass media are deceiving them, point out all the signs that we live under an empire of lies, and help spread awareness of what's really true and what's really possible.

All positive changes in human behavior of any scale are always preceded by an expansion of consciousness. Spreading awareness is the first step toward a healthy world, and we can each do that in our own small way every single day.

Featured image via Adobe Stock.

Ryan Grim
@ryangrim · Follow

Also @Hind_Gaza confirmed this is happening: the IDF has quadcopters luring people to them with recordings of the sound of women and children screaming, then firing on them

> **Mariam from Gaza** 🇵🇸 @KufiyyaPS
>
> I was the first person who talked about this, many didn't believe and said it was fake, anyways, 2 days ago someone managed to shoot a video and record the sounds
>
> An israeli quadcopter in the Nuseirat camp, makes the sounds of children and women to lure citizens from inside...

طائرة كواد كابتر إسرائيلية، بمخيم النصيرات ، تصدر أصوات أطفال ونساء لاستدراج المواطنين من داخل منازلهم

2:22 AM · Apr 19, 2024

The US Doesn't Support A Two–State Solution, It Just Supports Saying It Does
• Notes From The Edge Of The Narrative Matrix •

The US doesn't support a two-state solution, the US only supports saying the US supports a two-state solution. We know this because the US just vetoed Palestine's bid to become a full UN member state, after lobbying other countries to vote against the resolution—despite continually saying it supports the foundation of a Palestinian state. Washington's words say one thing, but its actions say the opposite.

This is because if the US admitted its actual position, it would greatly damage its reputation on the world stage. What the US actually wants is the same thing the Israelis want: for the Palestinians to go away, or lie down and submit completely, or otherwise stop being an inconvenience until they're a forgotten footnote in the dustbin of history. But the US can't come right out and say this, so it pretends to support a two-state solution that Israel has spent years doing everything it can to ensure never happens. It's a completely fictional resolution to a very real problem, but the alternative to supporting it is to admit you support continued apartheid, oppression, ethnic cleansing and genocide.

So the US maintains this ridiculous charade where it keeps pretending to support this fake non-solution, even while taking concrete actions which make it clear that it does not. Immediately after vetoing the Palestinian bid for UN membership, Deputy US Ambassador to the UN Robert Wood declared, "The United States continues to strongly support a two-state solution. This vote does not reflect opposition to Palestinian statehood," saying the emergence of a Palestinian state can only come about through direct negotiations between Israelis and Palestinians. We can see right now how things are going on that front.

As always, the only way to understand the US-centralized global power structure is to ignore what its officials say and watch what they actually do instead. This is good advice for understanding geopolitics and government dynamics in general, and it's good advice for sorting out fact from fiction when dealing with any manipulator in your personal life. Ignore their words, and watch their actions.

•

The Washington Post put out a good investigative report on the IDF's murder of six year-old Hind Rajab along with her family in Gaza earlier this year, showing that evidence points to Israeli forces being behind the attack. Washington Post editors immediately shitcoated this report by giving it the obnoxious headline "Palestinian paramedics said Israel gave them safe passage to save a 6-year-old girl in Gaza. They were all killed."

This headline is carefully crafted to suggest that Israel kindly granted safe passage to Palestinian healthcare workers, who were then killed by some unknown assailant. Imagine going through all the work of putting out a hard investigative report, and then having your editor slap this shit on it. Disgusting.

•

A senior US Air Force leader and whistleblower has informed Congress that the US is refusing to pull its military forces from Niger despite being told to do so by the new Nigerien government, and that refusing to withdraw troops from a nation where they aren't wanted is putting them at risk. Which means we've got yet another illegal US military occupation on our hands.

•

It's so stupid how everyone's felt the need to keep pretending to believe the Gaza death toll has legitimately hovered around thirty thousand for months now just because Israel supporters have even been calling the official death count a Hamas-driven exaggeration.

We all know the Gaza health ministry hasn't had the infrastructure or ability to count all the dead throughout the Gaza Strip for months and that the official number doesn't include people killed by starvation and disease due to the Israeli blockade, but because Israel supporters (including the US president) threw shade on the health ministry's numbers from the beginning they succeeded in dragging the Overton window all the way down to this ridiculously conservative estimate just through sheer vitriol and denialism—even though we know the killing never stopped.

Ralph Nader wrote in early March that the real number is probably more like 200,000. There's no good reason to discount this. It's certainly more likely than the number just continuing to sit around thirty thousand for no reason.

•

Hamza M Syed
@HamzaMSyed · Follow

U.S. at the UN: what we just voted no on is something that we strongly support

7:42 AM · Apr 19, 2024

1.1K   Reply   Copy link

Read 133 replies

Things That Have Been Discredited During The Destruction Of Gaza
• Notes From The Edge Of The Narrative Matrix •

List of things that have been discredited during the destruction of Gaza:

• Israel

• the "rules-based international order"

• liberals

• the label "antisemitism"

• the mainstream media

• Joe Biden

• the "two-state solution" myth

• Bernie Sanders

- Robert F Kennedy Jr

- the label "terrorist"

- the "human shields" lie

- the ADL

- AIPAC

- the US war machine

- right wing "free speech" supporters

- the Democratic Party

- the Republican Party

- Zionism

- all western governments

- all of western civilization

- everything westerners believe about their society

•

The US vetoed multiple UN ceasefire resolutions, then put forward a fake "ceasefire" resolution that didn't actually demand a ceasefire and accused Russia and China of "sabotaging" peace when they vetoed it, then an actual ceasefire resolution was passed which the US abstained from voting on rather than vetoing in order to save face over its Russia/China moralizing, and then the US declared (100% falsely) that the UN ceasefire resolution which passed is "non-binding".

•

Alexandria Ocasio-Cortez continues to support and defend Biden and just endorsed virulent Israel supporter Hakeem Jeffries for House Speaker, even after accusing Israel of genocide in a House floor speech.

If you say this is a genocide and then you support the people who are backing this genocide, it means either (A) you're fine with genocide or (B) you only called it a genocide to score progressive political points and don't actually believe what you said.

•

Biden supporters keep trying to spin his genocidal actions as some kind of aberration in his otherwise lovely behavior due to highly unusual circumstances, as though he hasn't been a bloodthirsty warmonger AND an extreme pro-Israel hawk his entire fucking political career.

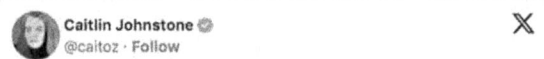

•

Caitlin Johnstone ✔
@caitoz · Follow
X

Israel's obsession with destroying hospitals makes no sense from a military strategic viewpoint but it makes tons of sense from a genocidal viewpoint.

Tameem | تميم @TameeOliveFern
Israel assaulted al-Shifa hospital [again] last week and the world did nothing, so it's assaulting another two hospitals now (al-Amal and Nasser).

The Daily Star

Published on 12:00 AM, March 25, 2024

Israel besieges two more Gaza hospitals

12:27 PM · Mar 25, 2024

10.2K   Reply   Copy link

Read 112 replies

Don't babble at me about how bad and wrong it is for Palestinians to use violence unless you can offer me a coherent plan for what they should do instead.

Civil disobedience won't work because Zionists have no conscience and don't care about Palestinian death and suffering.

The doors to a two-state solution with a real Palestinian state are slammed shut by Israel's political landscape and are being further bolted down by continually expanding settlements deliberately designed to prevent such a solution from ever emerging.

A one-state solution where everyone has equal rights and no ethnicity gets preferential treatment is an even more remote pipe dream which not even Israel's western allies support.

So what can the Palestinians do? It doesn't look like anyone who opposes armed resistance has any good answers. Really what they want is for Palestinians to just lie down and submit to whatever abuses Israel wants to inflict upon them and just slowly fade into obscurity and become a forgotten people, but they can't say that aloud without sounding like psychopaths so they just finger-wag at Hamas without ever offering any legitimate solutions.

Palestinians have been forced against their will into an impossibly horrible situation, and they sometimes use violence out of desperation because all the other doors are closed to them. If you want me to "condemn" them for this you can kiss my ass, especially since you can't even tell me what they should do instead.

•

The overwhelming majority of westerners spend roughly zero percent of their day thinking about Jews and Judaism, but because Israel stands accused of genocide people are being gaslighted into believing our society is overflowing with a widespread seething hatred of Jewish people.

•

All popular online posts about Israeli atrocities will have numerous comments underneath claiming that it didn't happen, or that it was justified, or that it was good actually, or that it should be blamed on Hamas. Every single one, without a single solitary exception. No matter how strong the evidence is. No matter how horrific the atrocity.

This shows you that Israel apologists don't care about truth or morality, and it shows you that they never have. All throughout Israel's history they've been lying and manipulating the public narrative about what the Israeli state has been doing this entire time. That's why they push so hard to get people de-platformed and censored and to get TikTok shut down: all they care about is controlling the public narrative, so they want to silence anyone who makes that harder for them.

Featured image via Gage Skidmore (CC BY-SA 2.0 DEED)

Israel Apologia Is One Big Fat Appeal To Emotion Fallacy
• Notes From The Edge Of The Narrative Matrix •

The Israeli hostages deserve far, far less interest and attention than the hundreds of thousands of Gazans who are being starved and murdered as we speak. The only way to believe otherwise is to believe Israeli lives are worth thousands of times more than Palestinian lives.

•

The PR campaign for Israel's destruction of Gaza revolves around encouraging everyone to focus on the feelings of people on the pro-Israel side instead of focusing on facts and evidence. The way Israelis are feeling about October 7. The way Israelis are feeling about the hostages. The way pro-Palestine demonstrations make western Jews feel inside. What feelings Biden is privately feeling toward Netanyahu. The whole thing's one big fat appeal to emotion fallacy.

Meanwhile the feelings of the two million Palestinians being starved, displaced, dismembered, traumatized, terrorized and having to watch their loved ones die horrific deaths right in front of them never features. We're discouraged from thinking about their emotions at all. Only the feelings of people who support these atrocities shall draw our attention and sympathy, thereby generating support for the continuation of those atrocities.

•

In December a former legal advisor to the State Department named Brian Finucane warned The Washington Post that the first Israeli attack on Al-Shifa Hospital back in November could be used as a precedent to "pre-excuse future operations against hospitals". Which is exactly what's ended up happening: Israel has since been obliterating hospitals throughout the enclave, and has attacked Al-Shifa three more times since then.

•

The propagandists who've been manufacturing public consent for this mass atrocity are just as guilty as the ones dropping the bombs.

•

Israel apologists will always have excuses and justifications for every horrible thing that comes out about what Israel is doing in Gaza. There is no testimony, investigative report, statistic or raw video clip that could come out showing horrific criminality on the part of the IDF or the Israeli state that would cause Israel supporters to go "Oh okay now this one really is bad, Israel needs to hold those responsible to account and make some dramatic systemic changes to make sure it never happens again."

This is because the function of Israel apologia (also known as hasbara) has never, ever been to promote truth or justice; its purpose has always been to promote and defend the information interests of the state of Israel. This is why no matter what Israel is exposed as having done you will always see prominent Israel apologists in politics and media as well as ordinary Israel apologists on social media providing excuses and justifications for it. They're not there to tell the truth, or to help the public understand what's happening, or to help create a more just and ethical world—their sole aim is to advance the information interests of their favorite ethnostate to ensure its continued support.

But the fact that so many thousands of people need to be working at this every single day shows how depraved Israel really is. Every genocidal regime in history has always had reasons and justifications for its behavior, and that's all Israel apologists are providing today. Don't take their manipulations seriously.

•

When I'm criticizing US aggressions toward Russia I get called a Kremlin agent a lot. When I'm criticizing US aggressions toward China I get called a CCP propagandist. Now I'm criticizing US/Israeli aggressions in Gaza and they say I'm an antisemite. At a certain point you figure out that there are just a lot of bootlickers out there who don't like it when you criticize the world's most powerful government, so they call you names.

That's all it ever is: vapid name-calling. It's what people do when they have no argument. When facts and morality are not on their side.

Featured image via Adobe Stock.

PROPAGANDA

Half Of Americans Have No Idea Whether Israelis Or Palestinians Are Suffering More Deaths

A new poll by the Pew Research Center has found that half of Americans have no idea whether more Israelis or Palestinians have died in the so-called "Israel-Hamas war".

"Most Americans report having strong emotional reactions to the Israel-Hamas war," the Pew Research Center writes. "Yet, for the most part, Americans are not paying very close attention to news about the conflict. One sign of this limited attention is that only about half of U.S. adults can correctly answer a question that tests their factual knowledge by asking whether the number of deaths in the war, so far, is higher among Palestinians or among Israelis."

The answer of course is that many, many times more Palestinians have died since October 7 than Israelis. There were reportedly 1,163 Israeli deaths on October 7 with the IDF claiming to have lost 246 troops in the ground offensive thereafter, while the Gaza Health Ministry says Palestinian deaths in Gaza are nearing 32,000 (arguably a massive underestimate).

An indictment of our media coverage.
pewresearch.org/2024/03/21/emo...

Most Americans report having strong emotional reactions to the Israel-Hamas war. Yet, for the most part, Americans are not paying very close attention to news about the conflict. One sign of this limited attention is that only about half of U.S. adults can correctly answer a question that tests their factual knowledge by asking whether the number of deaths in the war, so far, is higher among Palestinians or among Israelis. (The correct answer is that the death toll is higher among Palestinians.)

But the Pew Research Center is wrong to blame widespread American ignorance of these numbers solely on a lack of attention. The real culprit is the journalistic malpractice of the mass media.

The fact that half of Americans don't know whether Israelis or Palestinians are suffering more deaths in Gaza is the result of the appalling "Palestinian child walks into bullet"-style headlines the mainstream American press have been churning out since this conflict began.

Plenty of Americans are unfamiliar with the specific details of foreign conflicts their country is involved with, but because most of them encounter headlines and bits of information in their day to day lives there is a general awareness about things like the fact that Russia invaded Ukraine, or that 9/11 happened, or that the US went to war with Iraq amid claims of weapons of mass destruction.

But because the Israeli assault on Gaza is backed by the western empire, the headlines in the western press are a lot less clear about exactly what's happening there. In a new article for Declassified UK titled "How the Western Media Helped Build the Case for Genocide in Gaza", Jonathan Cook lays out numerous instances in which the mainstream press have brazenly misrepresented reality

about facts on the ground in Gaza in their headlines, like saying "food aid-related deaths" to describe an IDF massacre of Palestinian civilians waiting for food, or describing civilians being deliberately starved by Israel in ways that suggest they're just suffering from a natural famine.

In a society where only 20 percent of news consumers ever read past the headline, mass media propagandists know they can get away with a tremendous amount of manipulation of public consciousness by simply phrasing headlines in a way that advances the information interests of the US-centralized empire. If the mainstream press had been correctly informing the public that Israel is killing tens of thousands of Palestinian civilians and intentionally starving hundreds of thousands more, there would be no confusion among the American public about whether Israelis or Palestinians have been suffering more deaths since October.

American movies and TV shows like to make fun of nations like North Korea for having state propaganda, but Americans are easily the most propagandized population on earth. The propaganda of the mainstream press is so effective because Americans don't know it's propaganda, so they consume it without any distrust or skepticism.

That's just what's necessary to manufacture consent for the actions of the globe-spanning empire which revolves around the United States. There is too much power riding on the behavior of the US government for the American people to be permitted any real say in it, so their opinions and understanding are manipulated throughout their entire lives by state propaganda services disguised as news.

Featured image via Adobe Stock.

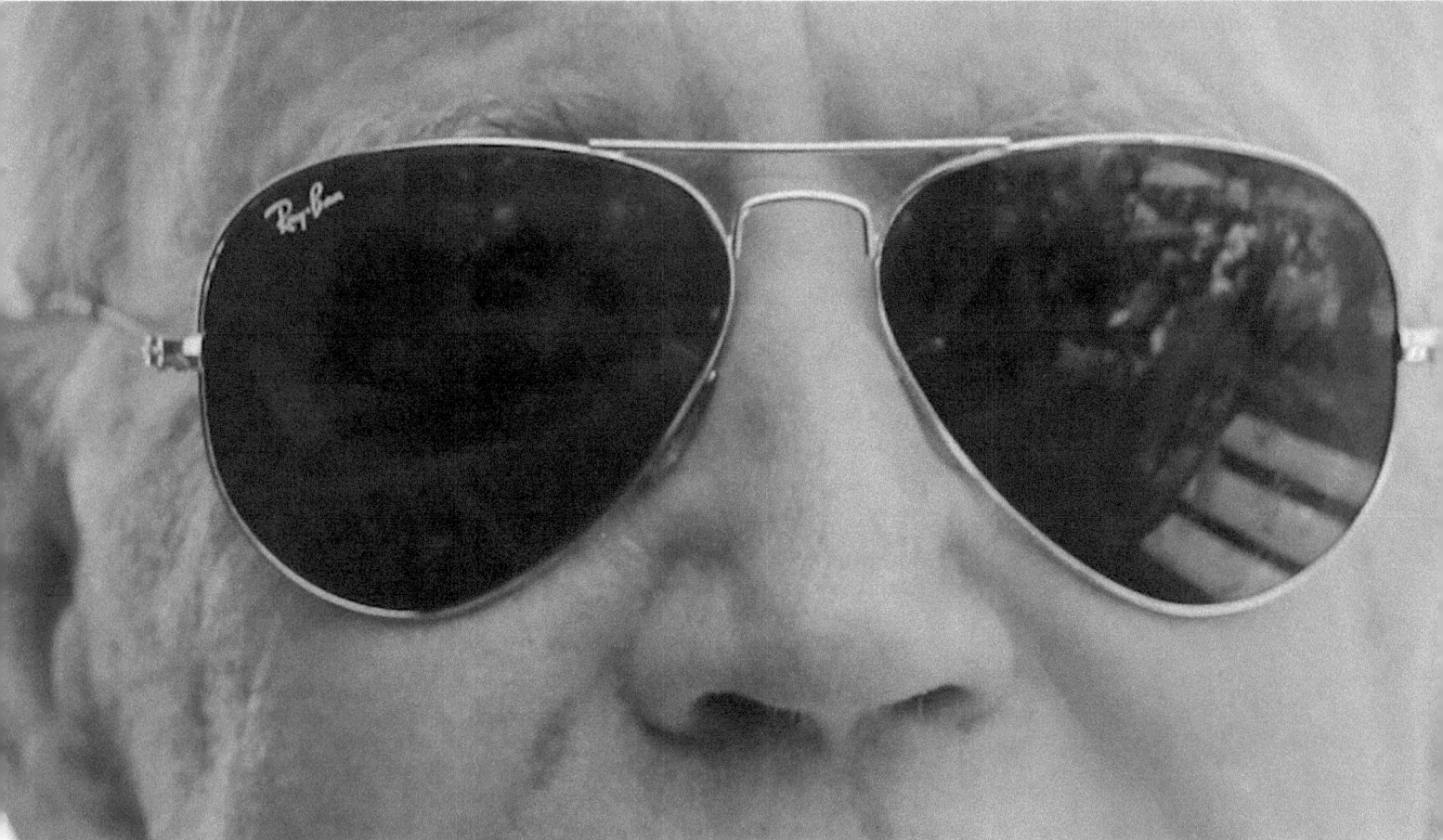

Aviator Sunglasses

Aviator sunglasses hide demented eyes
in a skull full of bank logos and forgotten AIPAC speeches,
boozy nights of rapefinger whisperings and Beltway balrogs,
and fundraising wisecracks with smiles made of Gaddafi's bones,
brain now crowded with paper shredders
and frantic, sweaty interns
staying up all night working
to dispose of the evidence.

Aviator sunglasses with glowing pentagons in them,
with mountains of skulls in them,
with dismembered children in them,
with gutted babies in them,
with screaming mothers in them,
with burning flesh in them,
with flattened neighborhoods in them,
crushed limbs sticking out of rubble in them,
fathers carrying tiny bags of body parts in them,
laughing, mocking, blood-soaked soldiers in them,
bombs and food falling from the sky together in them.

Demented eyes gazing out upon a dying world
through aviator sunglasses full of dead faces,
skin illuminated by a burning sky,
licking an ice cream cone
that is dripping deep red.

•

A Barely–Disguised Genocide
• Notes From The Edge Of The Narrative Matrix •

I just read a New York Times piece about the bodies that are trapped beneath the rubble in Gaza which said the Gaza Health Ministry estimates that there are 7,000 people listed as missing, but adds that that figure "has not been updated since November."

November. There is no chance that any of the numbers we're getting out of Gaza are up to date, including the death counts. Their infrastructure is shot and the scene there is just too chaotic. Nobody can keep track of anything anymore.

•

ISIS keeps attacking the enemies of the US and Israel for some strange and mysterious reason while funding for the main humanitarian group in Gaza gets cut due to completely unevidenced claims of Hamas affiliation. Re-fund UNRWA; de-fund ISIS.

•

It's funny to see the US proposing a fake UN "ceasefire" resolution which doesn't actually demand a ceasefire when it's public knowledge that the US could single-handedly create a ceasefire by telling Israel it will stop receiving US weapons if it doesn't negotiate one right now.

•

Ben Shapiro just cancel cultured Candace Owens out of a job for saying Palestinians are human beings and Alex Jones has condemned Israel's genocidal atrocities before most Democrats on Capitol Hill have. American right wing punditry is a trip, man.

•

It sure is a crazy coincidence how all this stuff about difficulty with food distribution, collateral damage, human shields, the need to eliminate Hamas etc just happens to combine to create a situation that looks exactly the same as committing a genocide against an undesirable population.

They're just doing a horrible thing they've wanted to do for ages and then using narrative to cover it up. Oh noes, it turns out it's really hard to get food and medical supplies to this undesirable population! Oh noes, it turns out the bad guys are hiding in the hospitals and the civilian infrastructure! Oh noes, it turns out the bad guys are hiding behind large numbers of women and children! Oh noes, it turns out we're going to need you all to move off of the land we've been coveting for generations!

It's a sick joke that not even a child would fall for, but you see western government officials and major news outlets treating it seriously every goddamn day. It's a barely-disguised genocide happening right out in the open, and the people responsible for telling the public what's going on in the world are pretending it's actually a very unfortunate series of highly convenient coincidences. There's an elephant in the room wearing a cardboard crown as a disguise, and they're all calling it Your Highness and telling everyone the king has come to visit.

•

Israel routinely massacres civilians who are waiting for food, attacks hospitals, picks off civilians with drones and snipers, and is deliberately starving the frailest and most defenseless people in Gaza to death, but the western political-media class keep calling this a "war".

•

People who wish to conflate Zionism with Jewishness often argue that most Jews are Zionists, but so what if they are? Most westerners are propaganda-addled imperialists, but if I didn't believe westerners can and do snap out of that worldview I wouldn't be doing what I do here.

In any system where people are being indoctrinated at mass scale by the powerful you're going to see the majority of that population buying into the indoctrination, but conflating the people with the political ideology they're indoctrinated with serves only to confuse and distort. If people had conflated "Nazism" with "Germany" that logic could have been used to justify exterminating every German after WWII, but because that distortion wasn't made it opened up the possibility of de-indoctrinating the nation from that pernicious worldview.

Betting on the possibility of a better future means drawing a distinction between the people and the unhealthy worldviews they've been indoctrinated with, whether that's Zionism, western imperialism, or anything else. We can only have a healthy world when the people snap out of their propaganda-induced coma and shake off the power-serving worldviews of this diseased civilization.

Featured image via Alisdare Hickson (CC BY-NC-ND 3.0 DEED)

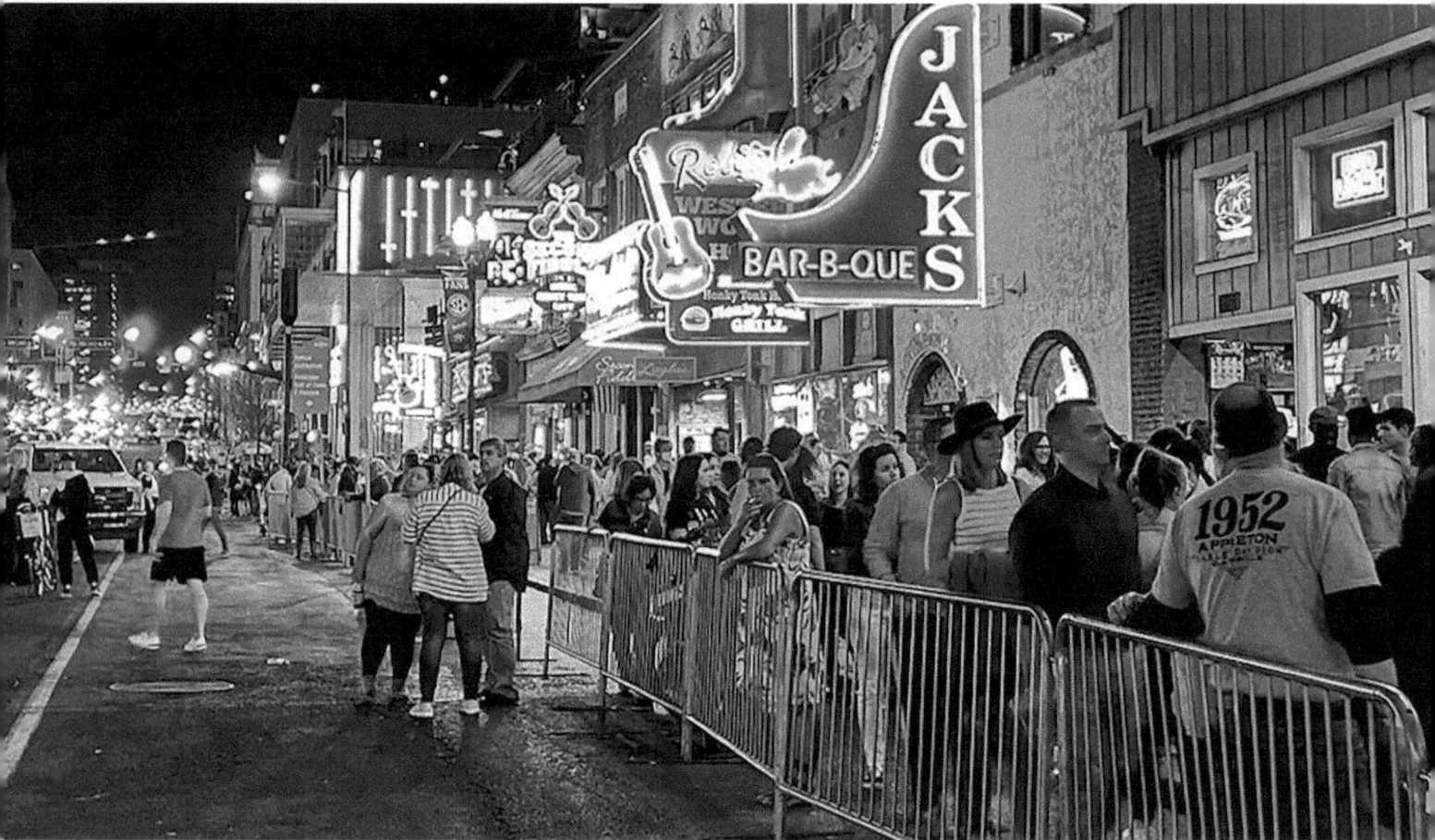

Ghost Town

Walking the streets of this ghost town, watching ghost people laugh and play and indulge like Gaza isn't burning, like children aren't starving, like people aren't dying slowly trapped under rubble next to the corpses of their loved ones, like IDF troops aren't merrily picking off civilians with drones and snipers while children get their limbs amputated without anaesthetic, with the full support of this ghost civilization and its ghost leaders.

This ghost town full of ghost cars, ghost buses, ghost trains, ghost pubs, ghost concerts, ghost theme parks, ghost cinemas, ghost festivals, ghost laughter, ghost feasting, ghost shopping, all going on just the same as it was before all this started. Little children running around with flesh on their bones and their organs inside their bodies like they're supposed to be, supervised by ghost parents with heads full of social clout and gossip.

Last month a man set himself on fire before the Israeli embassy and screamed "FREE PALESTINE" as he burned. He was not a ghost. He was flesh-and-blood real. He saw it. He responded to it. He treated this nightmare like the thing that it is.

We don't do that in this ghost town. We stare at screens and shovel snacks and booze into the gaping void within ourselves and flail our attention around looking for anything that will keep us from an even momentary encounter with the real. We do not look at Gaza. We look at everything except Gaza.

So we keep the charade going. Frantically keeping the gears of this ghost town turning like hamsters on a running wheel, running faster and faster because we can feel the wet mouth of authenticity nipping at our heels. It's like a giant theater improv game we're all playing together, where the whole instruction is to keep the scene in a constant state of frenetic motion.

Because we all know what will happen if we are still, on some level. We all know that stillness allows the smoke to clear and the mud to settle in the water, and from there it's only a matter of time before we find ourselves in the tyrannical grip of clarity. And then it will all bubble up. The lies. The phoniness. The discontentment. The feelings. Shame. Guilt. Truth. Gaza.

But there's only so long you can run from yourself. There's only so far you can flee before you get exhausted and fall down and find yourself staring up at the sky you've been living under your whole life. This fraudulent ghost town can't keep up this charade forever. None of this is sustainable. At some point and in some way, truth inevitably comes crashing in.

Featured image via Jonathan Cutrer (CC BY-NC 2.0 DEED)

The Empire Slowly Suffocates Assange Like It Slowly Suffocates All Its Enemies

The British High Court has ruled that WikiLeaks founder Julian Assange may potentially get a final appeal against extradition to the United States, but only within a very limited scope and only if specific conditions are met.

Consortium News @Consortiumnews · Follow X

Assange's Fate Awaits US 'Assurances'
consortiumnews.com/2024/03/26/ass...

The High Court on Tuesday rejected five Assange grounds for a new appeal, agreeing he had only three legitimate arguments but that the U.S. could nullify them with new "assurances," reports Joe Lauria.

12:29 AM · Mar 27, 2024

29   Reply   Copy link

Read 6 replies

The court ruled that Assange may appeal only on the grounds that his freedom of speech might be restricted in the US, and that there is a possibility he could receive the death penalty. If the US provides "assurances" that neither of these things will happen, then the trial moves to another phase where Assange's legal team may debate the merits of those assurances. If the US does not provide those assurances, then the limited appeal will move forward.

Absurdly, the court determined that Assange's lawyers may not argue against extradition on matters as self-evidently critical as the fact that the CIA plotted to assassinate him, or on the basis that he is being politically persecuted for the crime of inconvenient journalism.

The mass media are calling this a "reprieve", even "wonderful news", but as Jonathan Cook explains in his latest article "Assange's 'reprieve' is another lie, hiding the real goal of keeping him endlessly locked up," that's all a bunch of crap.

"The word 'reprieve' is there—just as the judges' headline ruling that some of the grounds of his appeal have been 'granted'—to conceal the fact that he is prisoner to an endless legal charade every bit as much as he is a prisoner in a Belmarsh cell," writes Cook. "In fact, today's ruling is yet further evidence that Assange is being denied due process and his most basic legal rights—as he has been for a decade or more."

Cook writes the following:

"*The case has always been about buying time. To disappear Assange from public view. To vilify him. To smash the revolutionary publishing platform he founded to help whistleblowers expose state crimes. To send a message to other journalists that the US can reach them wherever they live should they try to hold Washington to account for its criminality.*

"*And worst of all, to provide a final solution for the nuisance Assange had become for the global superpower by trapping him in an endless process of incarceration and trial that, if it is allowed to drag on long enough, will most likely kill him.*"

This kind of slow motion strangulation is how the empire operates all the time these days, across all spheres. Helping Israel starve Gaza while slowly pretending to work toward solutions. Drawing out a proxy war in Ukraine for as long as possible to bleed Russia. Slowly killing Assange in prison without trial under the pretense of judicial proceedings.

The US-centralized empire hunts not like a tiger, killing its prey with one fatal bite to the jugular, but more like a python: slowly suffocating the life out of its prey until it perishes. It favors the long, drawn-out, confusing strangulation of inconvenient populations and individuals, carried out under the cover of bureaucracy and propaganda spin. In today's world it prefers sanctions, blockades and long proxy conflicts over the big Hulk-smash ground invasions we saw it carry out in places like Iraq and Vietnam.

These slow suffocations can take more time, but what they lack in efficiency they make up for in the quality of perception management. It's bad PR to just openly invade countries and murder people, which is why the leaders of the western empire have been able to wag their fingers at Putin despite their being quantifiably far more murderous than Russia. People start snapping out of the propaganda matrix you spent so much time building for them and begin organizing against the political status quo your power is premised on.

Stella Assange #FreeAssangeNOW ✔
@Stella_Assange · Follow

Assange's 'reprieve' is another lie, hiding the real goal of keeping him endlessly locked up

@Jonathan_K_Cook

jonathan-cook.net/blog/2024-03-2...

10:56 AM · Mar 27, 2024

345   Reply   Copy link

Read 13 replies

So they opt for slow strangulation strategies where they can confuse the public about what's happening and who's responsible, outsourcing the blame to other parties while posing as the good guy who's trying to bring peace and stability. It takes time, but the empire has time to burn. That's what happens when you're the most powerful empire in the history of civilization; you have the luxury of biding your time while orchestrating large-scale, long-term operations to advance your power agendas.

Meanwhile Gaza starves, Ukraine bleeds, and Assange languishes in prison, each needing this to end with more urgency every day.

Featured image via Landjager (CC BY-NC 3.0 DEED)

Imagine If Russia Or China Did The Things Israel Is Doing In Gaza

Imagine how the western political-media class would be acting if Russia or China was bombing and starving a walled-in population of two million, half of them children. Seriously, imagine it. Imagine the rage and vitriol. Imagine the nonstop media coverage.

When Russia invaded Ukraine, US media coverage of that war exceeded the media coverage of all US wars in the previous three decades. If Russia were deliberately and systematically exterminating civilians in Ukraine or anywhere else, the western media coverage of those war crimes would be many times more.

It's almost cliché at this point to say "imagine if Russia or China did this", but such comparisons are important for retaining a sense of perspective on just how evil the western political-media class is being about Gaza right now. We're seeing articles come out in the mass media about starvation in Gaza which never once even mention the word "Israel". Do you think that would be happening if this were being perpetrated by a government which defies the western empire? Of course not.

Imagine how the western political-media class would be acting if Russia or China was deliberately blockading food from an imprisoned population of millions of people.

Imagine how the western political-media class would be acting if Russia or China was relentlessly raining military explosives on densely packed urban areas known to be full of children.

Imagine how the western political-media class would be acting if Russia or China was deliberately and methodically ethnically cleansing an oppressed population for entirely racist reasons.

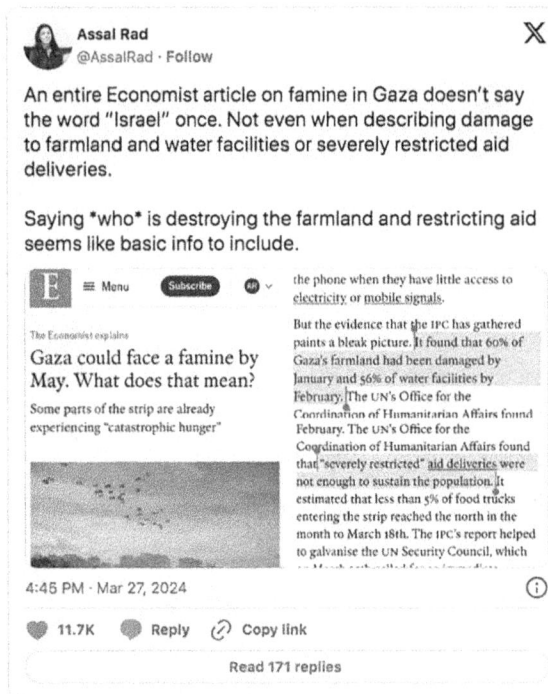

Assal Rad
@AssalRad · Follow

An entire Economist article on famine in Gaza doesn't say the word "Israel" once. Not even when describing damage to farmland and water facilities or severely restricted aid deliveries.

Saying *who* is destroying the farmland and restricting aid seems like basic info to include.

> The Economist explains
>
> Gaza could face a famine by May. What does that mean?
>
> Some parts of the strip are already experiencing "catastrophic hunger"
>
> the phone when they have little access to electricity or mobile signals.
>
> But the evidence that the IPC has gathered paints a bleak picture. It found that 60% of Gaza's farmland had been damaged by January and 56% of water facilities by February. The UN's Office for the Coordination of Humanitarian Affairs found February. The UN's Office for the Coordination of Humanitarian Affairs found that "severely restricted" aid deliveries were not enough to sustain the population. It estimated that less than 5% of food trucks entering the strip reached the north in the month to March 18th. The IPC's report helped to galvanise the UN Security Council, which

4:45 PM · Mar 27, 2024

♥ 11.7K   💬 Reply   🔗 Copy link

Read 171 replies

Imagine how the western political-media class would be acting if evidence that Russia or China are committing horrific war crimes was surfacing on a daily basis.

Imagine how the western political-media class would be acting if Russia or China were getting caught in lie after lie after lie while carrying out such a mass atrocity.

Imagine how the western political-media class would be acting if Russia or China tried to present them with blatantly fabricated evidence of crimes committed by the targeted population in justification of their atrocities.

We'd be living in a different political and media landscape. If Russia or China was doing what Israel is doing, entire presidential campaigns would have been built around who would oppose it most aggressively. Every sanction and embargo in the book would have been slammed upon the perpetrating government. The western press would be falling all over themselves to expose every atrocity and every lie and blaring those expositions as feature stories on every platform for months, and showering one another with awards for doing so.

Instead we get this. Government officials babbling nonstop about Israel's "right" to "defend itself" and how this would all be over if Hamas didn't keep fighting, while showering Israel with weapons to help it continue its atrocities. The mass media churning out a constant deluge of passive-language "Gazans are having trouble finding food for some reason" headlines and continuous reminders that this is all happening because of October 7, while repeating Israeli atrocity propaganda like it's gospel truth. All viable US presidential candidates vowing their unconditional support for Israel while occasionally impotently finger-wagging at this or that aspect of Israel's atrocities to avoid looking like complete psychopaths.

That contrast between how the western political-media class is acting toward the Gaza genocide and how we all know they'd be acting if an unaligned government was doing something similar is exactly why the US-centralized empire cannot be permitted to rule our world anymore. It pretends to stand for peace, justice, freedom and democracy, but in reality it just inflicts nonstop death and suffering upon human beings around the world and covers it up with propaganda spin from its servile mainstream press. It purports to uphold the "rules-based international order", but all that means in practice is that it upholds an international order in which the US empire makes up the rules as it goes along and changes them as it pleases.

Humanity cannot allow itself to be abused and tyrannized by this murderous, hypocritical globe-spanning power structure any longer. A better world is possible, but we're going to have to find a way to pry the talons of these monsters off the steering wheel first.

Featured image via Wikimedia Commons/Ministry of Defence of the Russian Federation (CC BY 4.0 DEED)

Violent Extremists Get Called "Moderates" By A Violent Extremist Empire

The imperial press have revealingly been using the words "moderate" and "centrist" to eulogize the warmongering former US senator Joe Lieberman, who passed away on Wednesday.

"Centrist former Sen. Joseph Lieberman has died at 82," reads a headline by NPR.

"As a moderate Democrat, Mr Lieberman developed a reputation in Washington for crossing party lines—as well as simply crossing members of his own party," says the BBC.

"Joe Lieberman, a former longtime Connecticut senator and moderate Democrat who became the first Jewish American nominated to a major party's presidential ticket as Al Gore's 2000 running mate, died Wednesday at age 82," writes The Wall Street Journal.

"Joe Lieberman, centrist senator and first Jew on major US presidential ticket, dies at 82," reads a headline from The Times of Israel.

Jacobin ✓
@jacobin · Follow

Joe Lieberman was a fairly unremarkable Washington politician who managed to get famous by becoming a particularly enthusiastic, inveterate warmonger and corporate marionette within the Democratic Party.

jacobin.com
The Extent of Joe Lieberman's Evildoing Was Truly Remarkable
Joe Lieberman was a fairly unremarkable Washington politician who managed to get famous by becoming a particularly enthusiastic, ...

7:02 AM · Mar 29, 2024

♡ 125   Reply   Copy link

Read 1 reply

Jon Schwarz
@schwarz · Follow

RIP Joe Lieberman. Not only did he lie about Iraq and WMD in 2003, he was still lying about it eight years later in 2011, and for extra credit did it in an incredibly smarmy and sexist way.

tinyrevolution.com/mt/archives/00...

January 20, 2011
Joe "Sweetheart" Lieberman's Long History of Lying About Iraq and WMD

8:39 AM · Mar 28, 2024

♡ 1.7K   Reply   Copy link

Read 34 replies

In reality, there was never anything moderate about Joe Lieberman. He was a violent extremist, who only looked like he walked a political center line through the lens of a violent extremist empire.

In an article titled "The Extent of Joe Lieberman's Evildoing Was Truly Remarkable", Branko Marcetic writes the following for Jacobin:

"Like most fiscal hawks, Lieberman is also an all-around hawk, unconcerned with government spending when it's in the service of bombing some far-off country or another. It's hard to find a war Lieberman hasn't supported, from both wars against Iraq (he was one of only ten Senate Democrats to vote for the first), to the Balkans in the '90s, to Afghanistan, Libya, Syria, Iran, Yemen, an ambiguous commitment in Ukraine, and many others.

"If you're a fan of the bloated, largely unaccountable centralized security bureaucracy of the Department of Homeland Security, thank Lieberman: he not only came up with the idea but introduced the legislation that created it. He also supported the terrifying appointments of John Bolton under both Bush and Donald Trump, citing his 'strong moral compass.'"

Beltway swamp monsters like Lieberman only get called "centrist" and "moderate" because they have ideological overlap with both of the increasingly indistinguishable mainstream political parties in the United States, both of which reliably support war, militarism, imperialism, capitalism, and oligarchy. Their differences are presented as massive by the imperial propaganda services known as the mainstream press to create the illusion of choice and competition, but they actually sit within an extremely narrow ideological bandwidth on the political spectrum.

One of the worst mistakes you can make when formulating your understanding of the world is to begin with the assumption that the truest and most accurate position must lie somewhere near the center of the two major political perspectives you see laid out all around you.

It's a mistake not only because assuming that the center position must be the best one is a type of fallacious reasoning known as the middle ground fallacy (the correct position between "Drink a gallon of bleach daily for good health" and "Drink zero bleach daily for good health" is not "Drink half a gallon of bleach daily for good health"); it's also a mistake because the entire framing arises from a situation that has been artificially engineered by the powerful.

It's a well-documented fact that the rich and powerful pour vast fortunes into manipulating the political and media landscape in ways that serve their interests. Their control over the news media and Silicon Valley tech platforms is used to set the agenda and influence public perception by determining what issues will receive attention and which won't in ways that preserve the political status quo they've built their empire upon, thereby shrinking the Overton window of acceptable debate down to a very narrow spectrum whose outcomes can't threaten their interests in any way.

This is what Noam Chomsky was talking about when he said "the smart way to keep people passive and obedient is to strictly limit the spectrum of acceptable opinion, but allow very lively debate within that spectrum." People assume there must be truth in the mainstream worldview because so many others are invested in the mainstream worldview, when really the only reason that worldview is mainstream in the first place is because so much wealth and influence has gone into making it mainstream.

The propaganda matrix can lull you into believing the false dichotomies of its two-party political framework because of how ubiquitous and widely believed it is and how aggressively it gets shoved in everyone's face from day to day, which can dupe you into losing sight of where a true moderate position might actually rest. One way to resist succumbing to this cognitive quicksand is to keep a clear vision of what a healthy world would actually look like, so that you are always acutely aware of just how far the mainstream worldview is from a sensible position.

Some time before he fatally self-immolated outside the Israeli embassy in protest of the US government's support for the Gaza genocide, Aaron Bushnell posted the following on Reddit:

"I've realized that a lot of the difference between me and my less radical friends is that they are less capable of imagining a better world than I am. I follow YouTubers like Andrewism that fill my head with concrete images of free, post-scarcity communities and it makes me so much more prepared to reject things about the current world, because I've imagined how things could be and that helps me see how extremely bullshit things are right now.

"What I'm trying to say is, it's so important to imagine a better world. Let your thoughts run wild with idealistic dreams of what the world should look like, and let the pain and anger at how it's not that way flow through you. Let it free your mind and fuel your rage against the machine.

"It's not too late for you or anyone. We can have the world of our dreams tomorrow, but we have to be willing to fight today."

It's valuable to hold a positive vision of what a truly healthy civilization would look like, because it's important to be clear on what it is you're fighting for. But it's also important because if you don't you leave an opening for these bastards to convince you to believe absurdities, like that Joe Lieberman was a moderate.

Featured image via Wikimedia Commons.

tiny thunder 🦋
@tinythunders · Follow

another aaron bushnell reddit response captured march 2023 via the wayback machine

I've realized that a lot of the difference between me and my less radical friends is that they are less capable of imagining a better world than I am. I follow YouTubers like Andrewism that fill my head with concrete images of free, post-scarcity communities and it makes me so much more prepared to reject things about the current world, because I've imagined how things could be and that helps me see how extremely bullshit things are right now.

What I'm trying to say is, it's so important to imagine a better world. Let your thoughts run wild with idealistic dreams of what the world *should* look like, and let the pain and anger at how it's not that way flow through you. Let it free your mind and fuel your rage against the machine.

It's not too late for you or anyone. We can have the world of our dreams tomorrow, but we have to be willing to fight today.

4:58 PM · Feb 28, 2024

💜 42.1K   Reply   Copy link

Read 219 replies

Israel Lies About Being A Victim So That It Can Victimize

• Notes From The Edge Of The Narrative Matrix •

The Washington Post reports that in recent days the Biden administration has quietly signed off on sending Israel billions of dollars worth of fighter jets and the 2,000-pound bombs that have been causing so much death and destruction in Gaza, even as Israel prepares to launch a bloody assault on the strip's densely-populated southernmost point.

Literally just completely ignore every single thing US officials say about the need to protect civilians and how Biden's feelings are privately "frustrated" with Netanyahu. Just ignore their entire narrative about what their goals are in Gaza. Their actions make it clear.

•

Protesters from Palestine Action have forced Israel-based arms dealer Elbit Systems to permanently close one of its factories in the UK as demonstrators have made it too difficult for the factory to operate. We'll never vote the empire away, but we might someday be able to direct action it away.

•

Video footage has surfaced of IDF troops murdering two unarmed Palestinians in cold blood and then burying their bodies with bulldozers to conceal their crime. This is surely not anywhere close to the first time such a thing has happened in Gaza, and is yet another sign that the death toll from this onslaught is probably a massive undercount.

Israel's assault on Gaza features heavy earth-moving equipment more extensively than any other military operation anyone's ever seen. One reason is because it's a great way to destroy Palestinian homes. Another reason is because it's a great way to hide dead Palestinian bodies.

•

An IDF commander has told Israeli media that on October 7 he made the decision to fire on vehicles he knew could have Israelis in them because "it's better to stop the abduction and that they not be taken," adding more weight to the mountain of evidence that Israeli troops fired on Israelis on October 7 to prevent them from being taken hostage. Israeli bombs and blockades have been picking off the remaining hostages ever since, with Israel now estimating that only 60 to 70 of the 134 hostages are still alive.

Whenever you run into an Israel apologist who is defending against criticisms of Israel's actions in Gaza by saying "Hamas just needs to release the hostages and this all ends," maybe go ahead and remind them of this.

•

ADL chief Jonathan Greenblatt just went on MSNBC's Morning Joe and compared wearing a Palestinian keffiyeh to wearing a Nazi armband. The mass media keep having this lunatic on as an expert analyst and he keeps saying the most bat shit insane things imaginable. Any screaming schizophrenic off the street would be just as qualified as Greenblatt.

•

Caitlin Johnstone ✓
@caitoz · Follow

X

"This is what our ruling class has decided will be normal."
~ Aaron Bushnell

Ali Jadallah @alijadallah66
Fadi Zant, aged 9, experiencing malnutrition, receives treatment after evacuated from the northern Gaza Strip to the IMC field hospital in Rafah. The Gaza Strip is on the brink of famine as Israeli attacks on the area enters its sixth month. (Photo by Ali Jadallah/Anadolu)

11:40 AM · Mar 28, 2024

Lowkey ✓
@Lowkey0nline · Follow

X

Israel's largest arms company, Elbit Systems, has permanently vacated its weapons factory in Tamworth, Staffordshire, following a relentless campaign by Palestine Action.

This is the third Elbit Systems site in the UK to be shut down permanently by Palestine Action.

2:13 AM · Mar 29, 2024

A former ranking IDF officer has told Haaretz that Israel is conducting "a war of cruel rich people" which is causing many times more destruction than necessary to accomplish its stated objectives against Hamas.

"In principle, it would be possible to arrive at similar achievements with 10 percent of the destruction we have caused," the unnamed source told Haaretz.

Ten percent. Israel is causing ten times more damage than it needs to to achieve its stated objectives because its stated objectives are false—Israel's real goal is not to defeat Hamas, it's to grab a bunch of land from a Palestinian territory.

•

Caitlin Johnstone ✅
@caitoz · Follow   𝕏

"This is all Benjamin Netanyahu's fault" has swiftly become the mantra of the western liberal political-media class. The idea is to pretend one guy was singularly responsible for the multinational effort to commit genocide in Gaza so that no big systemic changes need to be made.

> 🔵 **Louis Allday** @Louis_Allday
>
> No it's not—and what establishment 'journalists' like James O'Brien are doing is a transparent, cynical and desperate attempt to pin the blame for the genocide solely on Netanyahu in order to salvage the Zionist settler state's standing and perceived legitimacy. It won't work.

JAMES O'BRIEN
"THIS IS ALL BENJAMIN NETANYAHU'S FAULT"

10:39 PM · Mar 28, 2024   ⓘ

🤍 3K   💬 Reply   🔗 Copy link

Read 61 replies

Of all the pants-on-head idiotic things Israel and its apologists ask us to believe, "The UN just hates Israel for no good reason so all its claims should be dismissed" is definitely among the dumbest.

Israel apologists constantly claiming the UN is antisemitic and treats Israel unfairly remind you of a boy who never does any homework and keeps saying his bad grades are because his teacher hates him. The UN talks about Israel a lot because Israel is a murderous criminal regime.

•

If you still have any doubt that we live in a profoundly sick dystopia as deranged as anything that's ever been imagined in fiction, take note of the fact that the most powerful empire in history is currently trying to propagandize you into thinking an obvious genocide is fine.

•

They lied about decapitated babies so that they could kill babies.

They lied about rape so that they could rape.

They lied about Hamas using civilians as human shields so that they could use civilians as human targets.

They lie about being victims so that they can victimize.

Featured image via Adobe Stock.

Liberal Finger–Wagging At Netanyahu Is A Phony, Cynical Charade

We're seeing more and more of the cynical, obnoxious plan of the western liberal political-media class to try and pin the blame for the entire multinational genocidal campaign in Gaza solely on Israeli Prime Minister Benjamin Netanyahu.

"There is growing opposition to Netanyahu's war machine," reads a new tweet by Senator Bernie Sanders. "More Americans than ever are standing up against this horrific war in Gaza, which is causing tremendous suffering amongst the Palestinian people."

This is on the same day we learned that the Biden administration has quietly signed off on the delivery of billions of dollars worth of 2,000-pound bombs and warplanes for Israel to use in its ongoing massacres of civilians in Gaza. There is absolutely no excuse for continuing to babble about "Netanyahu's war" this far into a US-backed genocide. This is Biden's war as much as it is Netanyahu's—and Sanders supports Biden.

Sanders has been at this schtick for a while now, working to insert the idea into public consciousness that what we are seeing from Israel today is some kind of fluke aberration in the apartheid state's history and not the obvious fulfillment of its inbuilt nature. The other day he publicly griped that "the Israel of today is not the Israel of Golda Meir," falsely suggesting that there was once some kind of golden age in which Israel was not an abusive ethnostate built on ethnic cleansing, oppression, racism and injustice.

In an Al Jazeera article published earlier this month titled "This is not 'Netanyahu's war', it is Israel's genocide," Ahmad Ibsais berates Sanders and his fellow "progressive" senator Elizabeth Warren for this pernicious narrative control campaign, saying that "Blaming Israel's blatant human rights abuses, disregard for international law, and open celebration of war crimes on Netanyahu alone is nothing but a coping mechanism for liberals like Sanders and Warren."

Ibsais writes the following:

"*By blaming Netanyahu for the suffering and oppression of the Palestinian people, past and present, they keep alive the lie that Israel was built on progressive ideals, rather than ethnic cleansing.*

"*By blaming Netanyahu, they whitewash their seemingly unconditional support for a state blatantly committing war crimes and crimes against humanity.*

"*By blaming Netanyahu, and casting Israel as a progressive, well-meaning state that would respect international humanitarian law but is currently taken over by a bad leader, they are absolving themselves—and the US at large—of complicity in Israel's many war crimes.*"

But that's exactly what the Democratic Party has been trying to do in recent weeks. A couple of weeks ago Senate Majority Leader Chuck Schumer drew the ire of the Israeli right wing with a speech on the Senate floor saying that Netanyahu has become a "major obstacle to peace" who has allowed "his political survival to take precedence over the best interests of Israel," calling for new elections to oust the prime minister.

In a recent article for Jewish Currents titled "Chuck Schumer and Democrats' New Line on 'Netanyahu's War,'" Alex Kane picks apart the fallacious reasoning behind this trend:

> "But despite Democrats' repeated suggestion that Netanyahu is the impetus for Israel's war, political analysts say that in reality the prime minister's actions are in step with Israel's political mainstream. 'Schumer is operating in this fantasy that if you get rid of Netanyahu, you might be able to get somebody else who's more moderate who could then save the relationship between the US and Israel under the pretense of support for progressive values and democracy,' said Omar Baddar, a Palestinian American political analyst. But this narrative ignores how Israeli politicians almost across the board agree with Israel's conduct in Gaza, as do the majority of Israelis. Yair Lapid, the former prime minister and head of the Israeli opposition, supports the ongoing assault, as does war cabinet member Benny Gantz, Netanyahu's main political rival and the man who, according to polling, would become prime minister if Israel held elections today..."

> "Instead of constituting a substantive shift in US support for Israel, experts say, Democrats' emboldened critique of Netanyahu should be understood as an attempt to respond to growing voter frustration without changing policy, as the Biden administration remains unwilling to use US aid and arms exports to Israel as leverage to demand a change in behavior."

Louis Allday @Louis_Allday · Follow

No it's not—and what establishment 'journalists' like James O'Brien are doing is a transparent, cynical and desperate attempt to pin the blame for the genocide solely on Netanyahu in order to salvage the Zionist settler state's standing and perceived legitimacy. It won't work.

JAMES O'BRIEN "THIS IS ALL BENJAMIN NETANYAHU'S FAULT"

12:07 AM · Mar 28, 2024

626 Reply Copy link

Read 21 replies

Portuguese author and journalist Bruno Maçães recently tweeted that "One possible outcome of this is 200,000 Palestinians will be dead, Gaza will be destroyed, hundreds of thousand will be expelled and everyone will blame Netanyahu and move on."

AJOPINION

"The problem is not Netanyahu or any other Israeli politician or general. The problem is Israel's occupation [and] the settler colony.

Ahmad Ibsais
First generation Palestinian American and law student

Would it surprise you if this happened? Would it not be entirely in keeping with what we have been seeing from the US empire in recent years? Would it be very different from what happened after the US destroyed Iraq, blamed George W Bush and Dick Cheney, and then moved on without anyone having been held responsible or any meaningful policy changes implemented?

That's the entire goal here. The empire managers want nothing to change about Israel, nothing to change about Washington's relationship with Israel, nothing to change about US foreign policy or the US war machine in general, and for the mainstream public to be thrown some cognitive bone to chew on while the amnesia of the daily news cycle sets in.

They want everyone to pin all the blame for the Gaza genocide on Netanyahu, but this is not all the fault of Netanyahu. It's the fault of the entire Israeli state. It's the fault of Joe Biden. It's the fault of the Democrats. It's the fault of all the Israel supporters on Capitol Hill. It's the fault of the western press. It's the fault of the Israel lobby. It's the fault of the unelected empire managers in US government agencies. It's the fault of the entire US empire and all its imperial member states like Australia, the UK, the EU, and Canada.

Gaza is proof that the US empire cannot be permitted to exist any longer, and they're trying to get everyone to ignore this fact and blame the whole thing on one guy. Don't let them do this. Don't let them deceive you into losing sight of what they've done.

Featured image via Wikimedia Commons and Gage Skidmore.

AMERICANS

The Plan Is To Turn Palestine Into A Historical Footnote So It's Too Late To Save It

The Zionist plan for the Palestinians is to kill them and drive them off their land by whatever cruelty is necessary, with the understanding that one day people will look back on it in the same way they look back on the genocides of other indigenous populations, saying "Yeah it was bad, but that was in the past so there's nothing we can do about it."

The Zionists take a long view of history, understanding that all the outrage and backlash they're facing over Gaza right now will one day be irrelevant if they can carry out their plan for the territory today. They know that future generations of Israeli settlers will be able to say "Sure there was an ethnic cleansing in Gaza and a bunch of mass atrocities were committed, but that all happened before I was born; I had nothing to do with it. What do you want me to do, give up the home I've lived in all my life? That's nuts."

And they're absolutely right: if Israel succeeds in driving the Palestinians out of Gaza (and assuming humanity doesn't destroy itself via nuclear armageddon or environmental collapse), that is exactly the future they can expect to have. The genocidal atrocities against the Palestinians will be something kids learn about in history class. Israel itself might even be able to be a lot more honest about what happened, once the Palestinian problem has been fully resolved and the threat of a Palestinian state no longer exists.

So they do what they need to do in the meantime, with the understanding that this will one day all be rubbed away by the sands of time. They commit what atrocities they need to commit, they lie in whatever ways they need to lie, and they exert influence wherever they need to exert influence until they can get this thing locked down. Once they have, they can sit back and let old father time do the rest of the work for them.

That's why it's so important to oppose this thing now: because once Palestine is erased, it's highly unlikely that it can ever be restored. We see what an uphill battle it is to obtain any rights at all for indigenous populations in other nations founded on genocidal settler-colonialism, and they haven't even been driven out of their national borders into foreign countries.

The sins of the present and the recent past are much, much easier to correct than the sins of the distant past. That's why the Zionists are so keen to move these atrocities into the "sins of the distant past" category.

Featured image via Adobe Stock.

Israel's Savage Destruction Of Gaza's Healthcare System Is Exactly What It Looks Like

Israel has ended its assault on the al-Shifa Hospital in Gaza, because there is nothing left to assault. The facility—the largest medical complex in Gaza where hundreds of civilians had been sheltering—is now an empty, unusable, burnt-out husk. Witnesses report hundreds of corpses in and around the complex, with video footage showing human body parts protruding from the earth and bodies with zip ties on their wrists.

Israel is currently doing its usual song and dance where it claims the hospital was a Hamas headquarters and everyone it killed there was a "terrorist", but at this point the only people buying that schtick are the ones who desperately need to. This was a massacre of profound savagery. It's as plain as day to anyone who isn't deeply invested in pretending otherwise.

Tedros Adhanom Ghebreyesus ✓
@DrTedros

A @WHO team was on a humanitarian mission at Al-Aqsa Hospital in #Gaza, when a tent camp inside the hospital compound was hit by an Israeli airstrike today. Four people were killed and 17 injured. WHO staff are all accounted for.

The team was at the hospital assessing the needs and collecting incubators to be sent to the north of Gaza.

We again call for protection of patients, health personnel and humanitarian missions. The ongoing attacks and militarisation of hospitals must stop. International humanitarian law must be respected.

We urge parties to comply with the @UN Security Council resolution and ceasefire!

3:41 AM · Apr 1, 2024 · 290.8K Views

1,965 Reposts   **117** Quotes   **3,410** Likes   **147** Bookmarks

○   ⇄   ♡   🔖 147   ⬆

Dr. Mads Gilbert ✓   𝕏
@DrMadsGilbert · Follow

Today, we witness the total ISraeli destruction of the most important, 700 beds specialty hospital in Gaza, Al Shifa Medical Complex. It was established 78 years ago during the British Mandate, the name Shifa meaning 'The House of Healing'; now turned into a 'House of Death' by... Show more

6:47 PM · Apr 1, 2024   ⓘ

💜 679   ⚡ See the latest COVID-19 information on X

Read 47 replies

Israel, which at the beginning of the Gaza onslaught had adamantly denied that it would ever attack a hospital, has since launched hundreds of documented attacks on Gaza's healthcare services and has destroyed most of its healthcare system. Just today the director-general of the World Health Organization announced that an Israeli airstrike on Gaza's al-Aqsa Hospital compound killed four people and injured seventeen.

Oxford University professor Nick Maynard, who spent time working at al-Aqsa Hospital earlier this year, recently accused the IDF of "systematically targeting healthcare facilities, healthcare personnel and really dismantling the whole healthcare system" in Gaza.

"It's not just about targeting the buildings, it's about systematically destroying the infrastructure of the hospitals," says Maynard. "Destroying the oxygen tanks at the al-Shifa hospital, deliberately destroying the CT scanners and making it much more difficult to rebuild that infrastructure. If it was just targeting Hamas militants, why are they deliberately destroying the infrastructure of these institutions?"

Why indeed? If the objective is to target Hamas, why trash the hospital's medical equipment? If the objective is to target Hamas, why destroy the whole complex and make it unusable as a healthcare facility?

Logically we can only conclude that it isn't about targeting Hamas at all. It's about destroying Gaza's healthcare infrastructure.

Why would Israel want to destroy Gaza's healthcare infrastructure? The answer to that question has been clear for months: to make the land uninhabitable for the Palestinians. The same reason they're deliberately starving Gazans, destroying their homes, continually moving them from place to place and bombing every "safe zone" they create.

This is naturally giving rise to a situation in which the inhabitants of Gaza will either die or flee to some other country—which just so happens to be exactly what Israel wants them to do.

It's so obvious what's happening here. Painfully obvious. Poke-you-in-the-eyeballs obvious. But we're still subjected to a western political-media class who keeps forcefully telling us that this blatant ethnic cleansing campaign is not what it looks like. Telling us that all this starvation and destruction and elimination of healthcare services and the way it directly places pressure on the Palestinians to leave their homeland is just a series of coincidences arising from Israel's "war" of "defense". That only by pure happenstance does it look exactly the same as the advancement of an agenda that Israelis have sought to advance for generations.

Well I personally am through with having my intelligence insulted, and I hope you are too. The sky is blue, a spade's a spade, the emperor has no clothes, and Israel is conducting a very obvious ethnic cleansing campaign in Gaza.

Featured image via Adobe Stock.

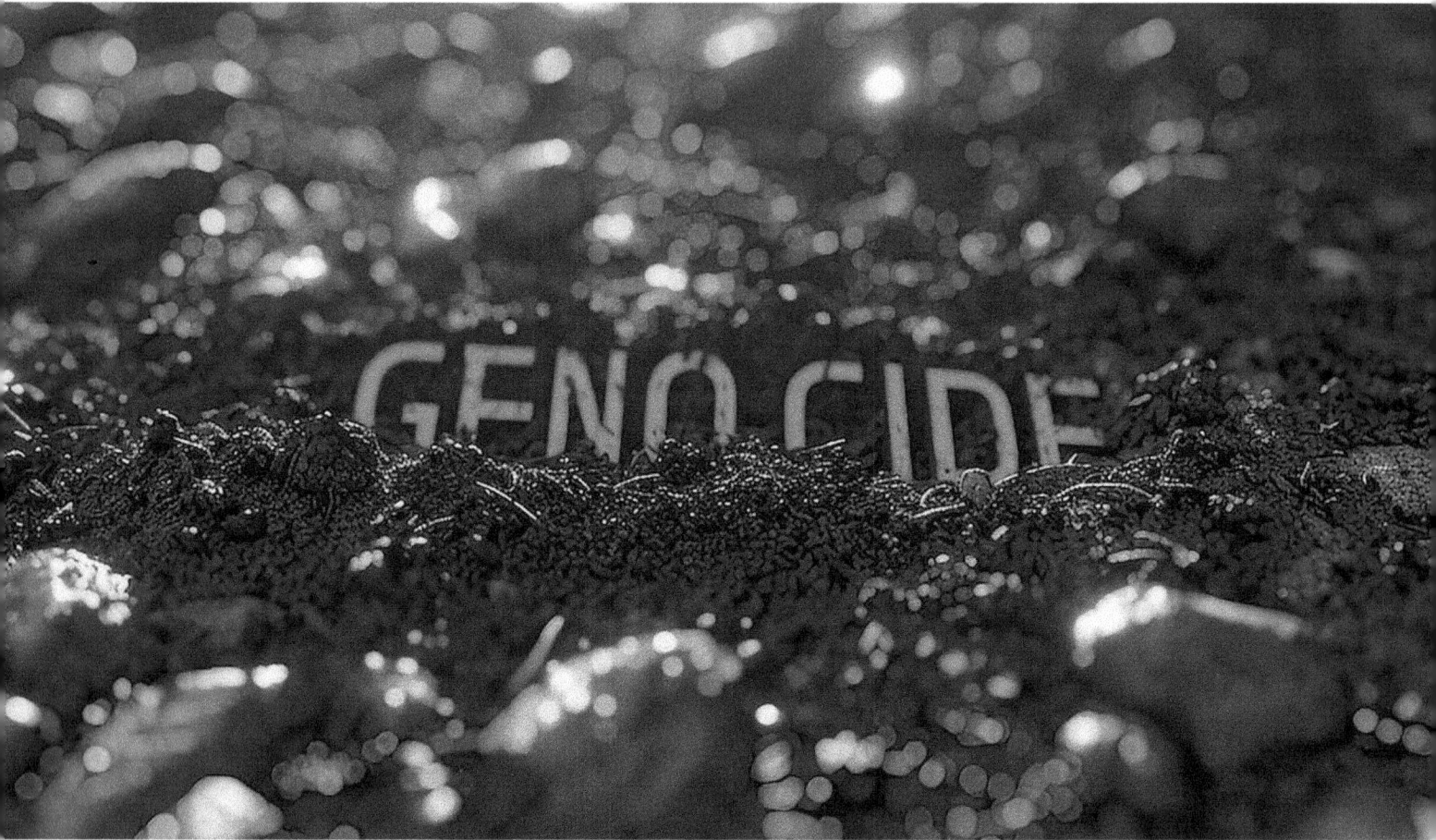

Israel Keeps Getting More Murderous
• Notes From The Edge Of The Narrative Matrix •

In the span of just a few hours we learned that Israel committed a horrific massacre at al-Shifa hospital, struck an Iranian consulate in Syria killing multiple Iranian military officers, and killed a vehicle full of international aid workers in an airstrike. This murderous regime is out of control.

•

Israel is so dedicated to protecting civilian life that it's deliberately gunning down unarmed Palestinians whenever they walk within firing range and then adding them to its "Hamas terrorists killed" tally. Haaretz reports that the IDF has set up "kill zones" in Gaza where they just shoot anything that moves, with an IDF reserve officer saying the number of Hamas members Israel claims to have killed is massively inflated because "In practice, a terrorist is anyone the IDF has killed in the areas in which its forces operate." Haaretz notes that the three escaped Israeli hostages the IDF gunned down in December had wandered into one of these kill zones.

•

A Doctors Without Borders physician went on Sky News to talk about Israel's deliberate destruction of Gaza's healthcare system, and the Murdoch shill anchor who was interviewing her asked her if Hamas was active in al-Shifa hospital fighting Israelis. The doctor, Tanya Haj-Hassan, told him "I am just shocked that we're still having this conversation" and went on to describe how Israel's assault on Gazan healthcare workers is so methodical that Gazan hospital staff have been changing out of their scrubs before leaving work because Israeli troops are picking off anyone in scrubs.

•

Saul Staniforth
@SaulStaniforth · Follow ✕

"Do you know if Hamas were there [in Al Shifa hospital]?"

@Tanyaalih: "I am just shocked that we're still having this conversation. [The Israelis] executed tens of people point blank, including one of our colleagues, Dr Ahmed Almaqadma, & his mother, who's also a physician"

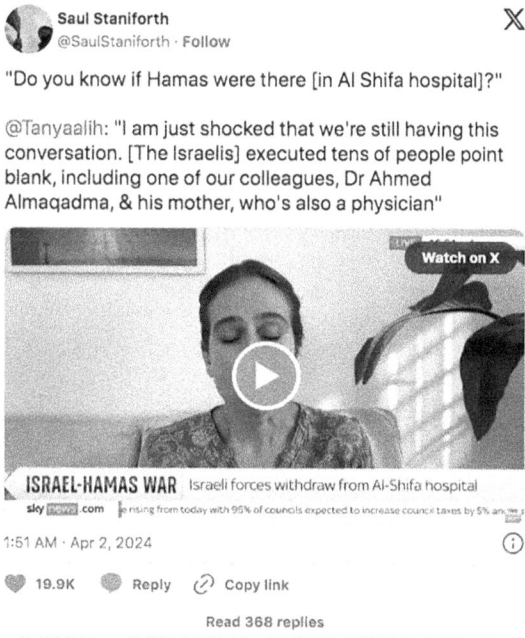

ISRAEL-HAMAS WAR Israeli forces withdraw from Al-Shifa hospital
sky news.com e rising from today with 95% of councils expected to increase council taxes by 5% an

1:51 AM · Apr 2, 2024 ⓘ

♥ 19.9K   Reply   Copy link

Read 368 replies

At the beginning of the year I tweeted, "Gaza is a live laboratory for the military industrial complex. Data is with absolute certainty being collected on all the newer weapons being field-tested on human bodies in Gaza (just like has been happening in Ukraine) to be used to benefit the war machine and arms industry." Since then we've learned that the IDF has been experimenting with new military robots in its Gaza assault, and that Israeli startups are now looking to start exporting new AI-powered war machinery marketed as having been "battle-tested" in Gaza.

•

Israel is a synthetic, artificially created state. It did not arise organically from the naturally existing conditions of the land and its people; it was unnaturally forced into existence by outside powers. It is more synthetic than meth. It is more synthetic than Pete Buttigieg.

•

Normal person: Stop doing genocide
Crazy person: But the TV told me rape happened six months ago

•

Netanyahu: [livestreams himself kicking a Palestinian baby off a cliff]

Netanyahu: [staring into camera] I kicked a Palestinian baby off a cliff because I hate Palestinians and I want to genocide them.

State Department press corps: Any comment on the video of Netanyahu kicking a Palestinian baby off a cliff and saying he wants to commit genocide?

State Department spokesman Matthew Miller: [smirking] Uh, I have seen that video, and I can say that we're looking into it and we're in touch with our counterparts in Israel on this issue. Beyond that I would only reiterate our position that claims that Israel is committing genocide are unfounded and anti-semitic in nature, and I have nothing further to add at this time.

•

Another one of the extremely stupid things Israel apologists ask us to believe is that Israel was right on the cusp of agreeing to give Palestinians a state before October 7, but because of October 7 that generous prospect is now off the table.

•

Rightists who see through the empire propaganda on the Ukraine proxy war but unquestioningly swallow all empire propaganda about Gaza are even dumber than people who've swallowed both, because they're just letting their favorite political faction do their thinking for them.

They're also dumber because they saw and understood that the mass media churn out propaganda constantly, but still assumed we're being told the truth about Gaza. They broke out of the propaganda matrix, then jacked their minds right back into it. They're like someone who pulled his head out of his ass, looked around, and then shoved it right back in.

If only the Democrats who rallied so aggressively against a fictional conspiracy between Trump and Russia could harness that same energy to oppose a real genocide by Biden and Israel.

•

Just ignore anyone who condemns Israel's genocidal atrocities in Gaza but still supports Biden. Their Israel-Palestine rhetoric is just for show.

Featured image via Adobe Stock.

•

I've been mentally referring to Matthew Miller as "Smirkula".

The 'Human Shields' Lie Has Been Conclusively, Irrefutably Debunked

One aspect of the recent revelations about the IDF's Lavender AI system that's not getting enough consideration is the fact that it is completely devastating to the narrative that Israel has been killing so many civilians in Gaza because Hamas uses "human shields".

If you missed this story, a major report from +972 revealed that Israel has been using an AI system called Lavender to compile kill lists of suspected members of Hamas and Palestinian Islamic Jihad which have been carried out with hardly any human verification. One automated system, psychopathically named "Where's Daddy?", tracks suspects to their homes so that they can be killed along with their entire families. The IDF has been knowingly killing 15 to 20 civilians at a time to kill one junior Hamas operative, and up to 100 civilians at a time to take out a senior official.

+972's Yuval Abraham writes the following:

> "Moreover, the Israeli army systematically attacked the targeted individuals while they were in their homes—usually at night while their whole families were present—rather than during the course of military activity. According to the sources, this was because, from what they regarded as an intelligence standpoint, it was easier to locate the individuals in their private houses. Additional automated systems, including one called 'Where's Daddy?' also revealed here for the first time, were used specifically to track the targeted individuals and carry out bombings when they had entered their family's residences."

> (Another +972 report by Abraham back in November revealed that IDF AI systems ensure that the Israeli military is fully aware of every child it's going to be killing in each airstrike, and that it deliberately targets civilian infrastructure as a matter of policy.)

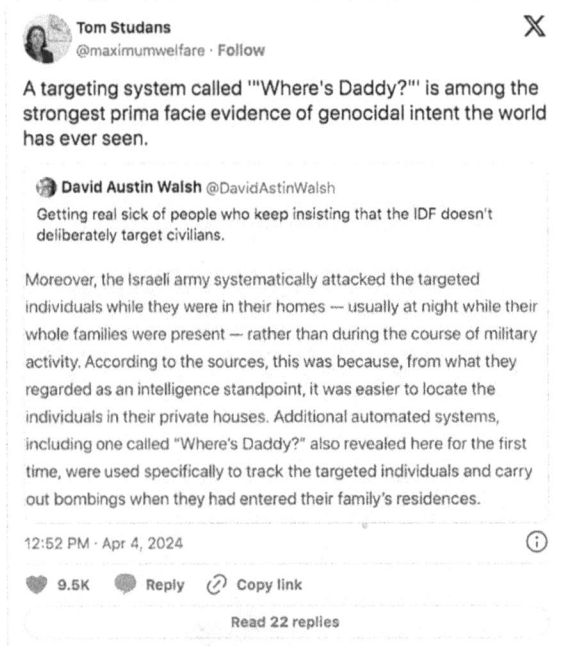

When questioned about these systems by +972, the IDF Spokesperson responded that "Hamas places its operatives and military assets in the heart of the civilian population, systematically uses the civilian population as human shields, and conducts fighting from within civilian structures, including sensitive sites such as hospitals, mosques, schools and UN facilities. The IDF is bound by and acts according to international law, directing its attacks only at military targets and military operatives."

The "human shields" narrative that's become so popular in Israel apologia insists that the reason the IDF kills so many civilians in its attacks on Gaza is because Hamas intentionally surrounds itself with noncombatants as a strategy to make the innocent Israelis reluctant to drop bombs on them. But as The Intercept's Ryan Grim recently observed on Twitter, this is soundly refuted by the revelation that Israel has been intentionally waiting to target suspected Hamas members when it knows they'll be surrounded by civilians.

"Israel's argument that they kill so many civilians because Hamas uses 'human shields' is torn apart by the revelation that the IDF prefers to attack its 'targets' when they are at home with their families," tweeted Grim. "It is not Hamas using human shields, it is Israel deliberately hunting families."

"A human shield is only a shield if your enemy values human life and seeks to minimize civilian deaths," Grim adds. "Israel deliberately maximizes the number of civilians it can kill by waiting until a target is with his entire family. Palestinians are not shields to Israel, they are all targets."

This is such an important point. Advocates for Palestine like Abby Martin have for years been presenting compelling arguments against Israel's "human shields" claims, and common sense shows that the presence of civilians is clearly not a deterrent to Israeli airstrikes, but because of these +972 revelations the lie has now been thoroughly, irrefutably debunked. Civilians aren't getting killed because Hamas hides behind them, civilians are getting killed because the IDF waits until suspected Hamas members are around civilians to target them with high-powered military explosives.

A popular quote attributed to former Israeli Prime Minister Golda Meir says "Someday we may be able to forgive the Arabs for killing our children, but we will never forgive them for making us kill their children." You see this quote pop up all the time in varying iterations, shared approvingly by Israel apologists around the world as though it's something wise and brilliant instead of a horrific defense of murdering children. But it turns out this morally depraved quote isn't even true by the most generous of interpretations: Israel isn't being "forced" to kill Palestinian children, it is knowingly choosing to.

The "human shields" narrative is just one more instance in which Israel pretends to be the victim while actually being the victimizer. They lied about beheaded babies so that they could get away with murdering babies. They lied about mass rapes so that they could get away with committing rape. They lied about Hamas using civilians as human shields so that they could kill civilians. They lie about being victims so that they can victimize.

Image by Adobe Stock

Six Months Of Hell On Earth

Six months of this now. Half a year.

Half a year of genocide apologia.

Half a year of the most outrageous lies you can possibly imagine.

Half a year of seeing children's bodies ripped to pieces and starved to skeletons on our social media feeds.

Half a year of atrocities justified by something that happened way back in October, and didn't even happen the way the news media tell us it happened.

Half a year of western government officials pretending obvious evidence of war crimes is just some ineffable mystery that we'll hopefully have answers to someday.

Half a year of Israeli officials openly stating their genocidal intentions in Hebrew for their Israeli audience and paying lip service to human rights and compassion in English for their western liberal audience.

Half a year of seeing reports that the IDF did something unbelievably evil, thinking "That can't be right, let me check it out," and then going "Oh, nope, it's actually even more evil than I thought."

Half a year of the western political-media class trying to frame the direct sponsorship of an active genocide as something other than what it is.

Half a year of passive-language "Palestinian child walks into bullet" headlines from the mainstream press.

Half a year of insulting our intelligence.

Half a year of insulting our humanity.

Half a year of unfathomable suffering.

Half a year of irreparable trauma.

Half a year of irreplaceable loss.

This fucking sucks, man. It sucks so bad. I've always enjoyed doing commentary on the crimes of the empire, but these last six months have been truly harrowing. It's awful having to stare directly at hell on earth from day to day with compassion in your heart. The only thing keeping this project going is the fact that it needs to be done, and the knowledge that my own suffering isn't the faintest shadow of what the Palestinians are going through right now.

This needs to end. It needs to end with desperate urgency. But we're seeing no signs that it's about to.

I don't have anything wise or insightful to add to any of this right now. Some days all you can do is point to the nightmare and call it what it is, and we can all just be real about reality and feel our feelings about that.

I guess all I can really say is that at least we're not alone in seeing what we're seeing. The whole world is watching Israel commit a horrifying mass atrocity backed by the full might of the empire, and more and more eyes are opening to the reality of what this means for their society and everything they've been told to believe about it.

Every positive change in human behavior is always preceded by an expansion of consciousness, and Gaza is expanding western consciousness like nothing ever before.

So at least there's that. At least there's the possibility that something good might one day grow out of this steaming pile of shit.

And that's all I've got for you. That's the best I can do right now.

Featured image via Adobe Stock.

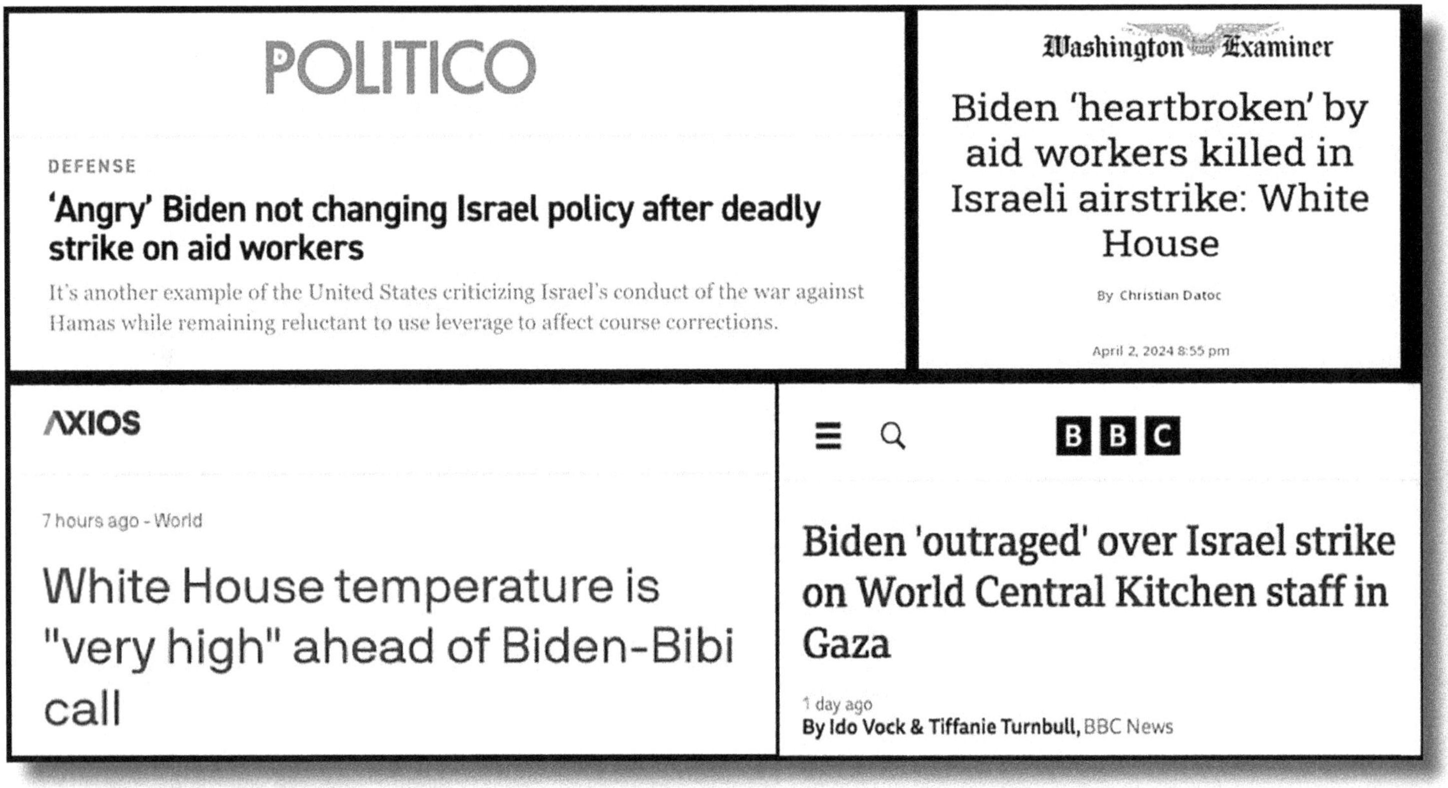

POLITICO

DEFENSE

'Angry' Biden not changing Israel policy after deadly strike on aid workers

It's another example of the United States criticizing Israel's conduct of the war against Hamas while remaining reluctant to use leverage to affect course corrections.

Washington Examiner

Biden 'heartbroken' by aid workers killed in Israeli airstrike: White House

By Christian Datoc

April 2, 2024 8:55 pm

AXIOS

7 hours ago - World

White House temperature is "very high" ahead of Biden-Bibi call

☰ Q **BBC**

Biden 'outraged' over Israel strike on World Central Kitchen staff in Gaza

1 day ago
By Ido Vock & Tiffanie Turnbull, BBC News

Stop Reporting On Biden's Angry Feelings Toward Israel. It's Not News. It's Not Interesting.

The imperial media cannot stop babbling about how angry President Biden's feelings are feeling toward Israel like it's some kind of actual news story, even as this administration cheerfully pours mountains of weaponry into backing Israel's genocidal atrocities in Gaza.

If you haven't been following the mass media's coverage of Biden and Gaza for the last six months, the entire thing can be summed up by the headline of a new Politico article, "'Angry' Biden not changing Israel policy after deadly strike on aid workers".

This is in reference to the Israeli military's deliberate assassination of seven World Central Kitchen aid workers, which conveniently resulted in multiple humanitarian aid organizations ceasing their operations in Gaza out of fear of being attacked themselves. The attack has been drawing widespread condemnation throughout the western world, because six of the workers killed came from western nations and are therefore considered real human

Eli Valley
@elivalley · Follow

Israel used an automated system called "Where's Daddy?" to ensure it killed AI-designated targets while the targets were at home with their spouses and children:

972mag.com
'Lavender': The AI machine directing Israel's bombing spree in Gaza
The Israeli army has marked tens of thousands of Gazans as suspects for assassination, using an AI targeting system with little human ...

4:13 AM · Apr 4, 2024

♥ 7K   💬 Reply   🔗 Copy link

Read 95 replies

Dave DeCamp ✓
@DecampDave · Follow

"I'm so angry I can barely sign off on this 2,000 pound bomb shipment"

🔵 **POLITICO** ✓ @politico

'Angry' Biden not changing Israel policy after deadly strike on aid workers ow.ly/I48H105olOl

7:41 AM · Apr 4, 2024

♥ 949   💬 Reply   🔗 Copy link

Read 12 replies

beings by the western empire. Biden released a statement saying how "outraged and heartbroken" he is about the incident, drawing a fresh deluge of frenzied reporting about how the president's feelings are feeling about Israel.

But as the aforementioned Politico article illustrates, none of this actually matters because this administration's Israel policy has not changed. Biden is reportedly set to greenlight a sale of fighter jets to Israel in a deal worth $18 billion, and this is just a few days after we learned that this administration has quietly signed off on the delivery of more of the 2,000-pound bombs with which the IDF has been obliterating so many civilians in Gaza. The Biden White House still adamantly refuses to acknowledge that Israel has even once violated humanitarian law these past six months.

So why are we being told by the news media over and over and over again that Biden is super duper upset with the government of Israel? It doesn't matter. At all. It's not a news story. It's not interesting. Nobody with functioning gray matter between their ears gives the tiniest sliver of a fuck. But they've been hammering and hammering and hammering on this idiotic narrative for months.

The answer of course is because the western news media are propaganda services for the western empire of which Washington is the central hub, and their job is therefore to make the US government look good. By emphasizing the point over and over and over again that the US president strongly disapproves of the Israeli regime's behavior in Gaza, the imperial spinmeisters are distancing the White House from one of the darker chapters in the history of the United States even as Biden signs off on this mass atrocity day after day despite being fully capable of ending it at any time.

This fuzzbrained nonsense is happening at the same time a major report from +972 reveals that Israel has been using an AI system to compile kill lists of suspected members of Hamas and Palestinian Islamic Jihad which have been carried out with hardly any human verification. One automated system, psychopathically named "Where's Daddy?", tracks suspects to their homes so that they can be killed along with their entire families. The IDF has been knowingly killing 15 to 20 civilians at a time to kill one junior Hamas operative, and up to 100 civilians at a time to take out a senior official.

This is the kind of murderous depravity that the Biden administration has been giving the thumbs up to day after day for half a year now while the imperial media prattle on like preschoolers about the president's feelings.

Stop telling us about the president's feelings. Stop telling us he's "angry" and "frustrated" with Israel. No one cares. Nobody gives a shit how Biden's feelings feel about the government he's helping carry out a genocide. All that matters is that he's helping them commit genocide.

This six-month mass atrocity has been one nonstop insult to our intelligence.

•

Israel Lets Some Aid Into Gaza So The US Will Keep Giving It Weapons To Kill People In Gaza
• Notes From The Edge Of The Narrative Matrix •

Israel has generously and compassionately reopened the Erez crossing to allow aid into Gaza, as it is the only way to ensure that the US will keep sending them weapons to kill the people in Gaza.

Biden sent Netanyahu one warning about a failure to protect civilians possibly costing Israel its US support and the crossing opened immediately, which proves (A) that Israel has been intentionally starving Gazans by closing entrances off from aid and (B) that Biden could have ordered this to stop at any time.

•

The Biden administration approved another weapons package for Israel on the same day Israel killed a bunch of international aid workers in Gaza and bombed the Iranian consulate in Syria. But please, tell me more about how frustrated and angry and outraged and upset Biden's feelings are feeling toward Israel.

•

Caitlin Johnstone ✓
@caitoz · Follow

X

Pretty ballsy to say "there's no way in hell Israel would do something bad" six months into a genocide.

Karol Markowicz ✓ @karol
There's no way in hell IDF targeted aid workers and everyone, including the enemies of Israel, know this.

10:20 PM · Apr 3, 2024

ⓘ

❤ 23.1K   💬 Reply   🔗 Copy link

Read 117 replies

•

The huge amount of western outrage and sympathy we're seeing over the IDF assassination of an international aid convoy compared to the systematic extermination of Palestinians we've seen over the last six months confirms the west only regards white people as full human beings, which is a point we'd already seen driven home by the disproportionate amount of outrage and sympathy we saw over Ukraine.

But you know what? We'll take it. Things are that desperate that if you can only support an end to the Gaza genocide if you see six westerners get killed, I say welcome aboard anyway. Hopefully this is the beginning of the formation of an actual conscience that's worth a damn.

•

The mass media are reporting that the preliminary IDF debrief into the killing of several World Central Kitchen employees in Gaza has found that the multiple strikes were not carried out with the intention of killing those workers, a report which if you ask me has big "CIA Says It Has Found No Link Between Itself and Crack Trade" energy.

•

Haaretz has a new article out titled "At Singapore Airshow, the Gaza War Was a Selling Point for Israeli Weapon Manufacturers," which is exactly what it sounds like. One of the ugliest things about this dystopia is that acts of mass military slaughter are always immensely profitable for a specific industry. They're profitable in and of themselves, even before you add in things like land and resource grabs, just by helping to market and sell more weapons.

•

Stop calling this a "war". A war doesn't involve conversations about whether or not a walled-in population should be allowed to have food, medicine and electricity. If you have that much control over a population, you can't be at war with it. You're just killing a bunch of prisoners.

•

Biden and his cohorts aren't mad at Netanyahu for committing a genocide, they're mad at Netanyahu for not hiding a genocide.

•

I've fucking had it with people who blindly regurgitate empire propaganda about Gaza. Fuck right off with your weaponized gullibility.

•

The thing that's so pathetic about the push to blame this whole mass atrocity on Netanyahu is that the people doing this aren't even really going after Netanyahu. They're not pushing to send him to The Hague and have him imprisoned for war crimes or bring about any meaningful consequences at all—they're just saying we should feel negative feelings toward him for a bit like we did with Bush.

It's always about feelings with the imperial spin campaign over Gaza. Biden's feelings toward Netanyahu, Israeli feelings about October 7, the feelings of western Jews about pro-Palestine protests. The whole thing's been one nonstop appeal to emotion fallacy.

•

MAGA Republicans claim to be a bold anti-war, anti-establishment faction, which is squarely refuted by their support for the Gaza genocide.

Democrats claim to support human rights and to oppose tyranny and racism, which is squarely refuted by their support for the Gaza genocide.

Image by Adobe Stock.

Dancing Outside The Concentration Camp

Dancing outside the concentration camp,
rave music pounding through our bones like bombs.
A disco at the genocide, baby.
A disco at the genocide.
Twerking outside the open-air prison.
Raving while Gaza asphyxiates.
Twirling glow sticks while a Final Solution is planned.
Just an innocent bit of fun.
Chill out and dance outside the concentration camp.
What could possibly go wrong?
We've got the IDF looking after us.
They'd never let anything bad happen.
So dance while the Palestinians are squeezed to death.
Dance while the polar ice caps melt.
Dance while the oceans fill with plastic.
Dance while the rainforests disappear.
Dance while nuclear warheads are primed.
Dance while mothers scream impossible screams.
Dance while the arms industry reaps record profits.
Dance while fathers pick up pieces of their kids.
Dance while AI helps exterminate families.
Dance while Gazans dehydrate under rubble.
Dance while limbs are amputated without anaesthesia.
Dance while death machines patrol the sky.
Dance while the news man fills our heads with lies.
Dance while the podium man denies everything he sees.
Dance while the sharptooth manipulators scheme.
Dance while our minds are turned into machines.
Dance to the beat of imperial psytrance.
Dance to the beat of the Pentagon Polka.
What could possibly go wrong?
Dance outside the concentration camp.
A disco at the genocide, baby.
A disco at the genocide.

•

As Support For Gaza Goes Mainstream, Don't Let The Empire Co-Opt The Movement

Opposition to the slaughter in Gaza appears to be getting more mainstream, which is obviously great, but when political impulses go mainstream it means there's going to be a massive and concerted effort to funnel public sentiment in a direction that doesn't damage the interests of the empire.

𝕏

Blinken: Israel Becoming 'Indistinguishable' From Hamas
America's top diplomat said Israel would have to allow an
increase in aid shipments to Gaza to meet US demands
by Kyle Anzalone
@KyleAnzalone_ #Blinken #Gaza #Israel #Hamas
#wckitchen
news.antiwar.com/2024/04/05/bli... Show more

7:09 AM · Apr 6, 2024   ⓘ

♥ 55   💬 Reply   ⟋ Copy link

Read 18 replies

They're going to try to blame this all on Netanyahu.

They're going to insist that Israel itself is fine and the only thing that went wrong was a fluke incident in which an aberrational right wing faction briefly got into power.

They're going to try to wash the western empire's hands of the mass atrocities it directly facilitated in Gaza.

They're going to try to frame Biden as a basically decent politician who found himself trapped in an impossible situation.

They're going to keep pretending a two-state solution is right around the corner and doing everything they can to stall out meaningful change on Palestinian rights, while blaming any obstacles to peace on the Palestinian resistance.

They're going to pollute the information ecosystem with a deluge of messaging which is all designed to counter the notion that Gaza means the entire status quo needs to be overhauled—with regard to Israel-Palestine, with regard to US foreign policy, with regard to the US government itself, and with regard to the western power structure in general.

They're going to say everything they need to say to ensure that everyone understands that the basic status quo in Israel, the United States and the western world is working perfectly fine, and this was all just an innocent little oopsie poopsie caused by a few bad apples.

They'll justify, they'll excuse, they'll exonerate, and then they'll distract, moving public attention on to the next big thing and allowing the amnesia of the daily news churn to wash Gaza from our attention—all while pretending to be on our side.

Guns are Post-Birth Abortifacients
@ritaresarian · Follow

𝕏

They killed a white American and passive voice died instantly

AP **The Associated Press** ✓ @AP
Rights group says Israeli strike on Gaza building killed 106 in apparent war crime apnews.com/article/israel...

2:41 AM · Apr 6, 2024   ⓘ

♥ 61.5K   💬 Reply   ⟋ Copy link

Read 50 replies

Mohammad Alsaafin
@malsaafin · Follow

It's absolutely a good thing these stories are getting mainstream coverage in the US now.

It's also...weird...seeing stories that have been all over social media for months suddenly break into that ecosystem all of a sudden.

> **NBC News** ⊘ @NBCNews
>
> Gaza's universities embodied the ambitions of young Palestinians.
>
> In weeks, the Israeli military destroyed them.
> nbcnews.app.link/nLNnEi5Vwlb

1:03 PM · Apr 6, 2024

♥ 3.4K   Reply   🔗 Copy link

Read 28 replies

This messaging will need to be fought tooth and claw. We cannot allow them to neuter this political moment with spin and propaganda. We need to make sure their criminality remains front and center of public awareness, and we need to push for the real revolutionary changes that Gaza plainly proves are needed.

Let mainstream sentiment turn against the current Israeli regime and bring an end to the butchery in Gaza, but don't let the imperial narrative managers co-opt anything. Don't let them hijack the zeitgeist that's been building.

View all words and actions of the western political-media class with aggressive skepticism, and push back forcefully every time they try to push public sentiment in a direction that advantages the empire.

Featured image via Mark McGuire (CC BY 3.0 NZ)

Australian Military Refuses To Disclose Arms Deal With Israel To Protect Its 'Reputation'

Australia's Defence Department has refused a Freedom of Information request about the details of an arms deal with Israel on the grounds that such information "could harm Australia's international standing and reputation," which suggests the details must be pretty damning. Equally as scandalous, this refusal was reportedly made in consultation with the Israeli government.

In an article titled "Details of defence deal with Israel kept under wraps to protect Australia's 'reputation'," the ABC's Andrew Greene details how the Australian military snubbed a Freedom of Information request by the Australian Greens regarding a "Memorandum of Understanding" between Australia and Israel that was signed in 2017.

"The document within the scope of this request contains information which, if released, could reasonably be expected to damage the international relations of the Commonwealth," the Defence Department said in a letter explaining its rejection.

"A summary provided by the Australian Information Commissioner (OAIC) to the Greens reveals that the Israeli government was also consulted about releasing the document before Defence ultimately rejected the FOI request," the ABC reports.

"The document contains information communicated to Australia by a foreign government and its officials under the expectation that it would not be disclosed," a Defence official wrote in justification of its decision.

Greens senator David Shoebridge objected, saying "There is no place for secret arms treaties and secret arms deals between countries, and there is certainly no place for giving other countries veto power over what the Australian government tells the public about our government's defence and arms deals."

"Over 30,000 people have been killed by the State of Israel in Gaza in the past six months. In this context, the Australian public has a right to know about the military trade relationship with the State of Israel," added Shoebridge.

AWPR
@WarPowersReform · Follow

Details of defence deal with Israel kept under wraps to protect Australia's 'reputation'

"There is no place for secret arms treaties and secret arms deals between countries,"

#auspol

abc.net.au
Details of defence deal with Israel kept under wraps to protect Austral...
Details of an agreement struck between Australia and Israel on defence industry cooperation will not be released publicly over concerns the ...

11:11 AM · Apr 9, 2024

♥ 10   Reply   Copy link

Read 1 reply

It's wild to think about the fact that the Australian warmakers determined this admission, that the truth would harm Australia's reputation, to be the option that was least destructive to Australia's reputation. When someone tells you "I can't tell you the truth about that because the truth will make everyone

David Shoebridge
@DavidShoebridge · Follow

Australia has a secret defence industry cooperation deal with Israel and you're not allowed to know what's in it because apparently Israel has a veto on Australian FOI!?

Why, and what, are they hiding?

7:01 AM · Apr 9, 2024

♥ 1.3K   Reply   Copy link

Read 94 replies

dislike me," it means they've ruled out every other option before coming to that position because the truth really is that ugly.

It's like coming home to find your husband frantically burning clothes and mopping up blood and asking him what's going on, and he says "I can't tell you because the truth would harm your opinion of me." Your very first thought after that is going to be that he must have done something very, very bad if that's the best answer he could give you.

Back in November lawyer and researcher Kelly Trantner published an article with Declassified Australia titled "Australia's role in the bombing of Gaza" about Israel's use of Australian equipment to conduct its F-35 bombing campaigns, writing that "no bombs could be dropped on Gaza by an F-35 without parts manufactured for the F-35s by Melbourne company, Rosebank Engineering."

Trantner notes that more than 70 Australian companies have been awarded "over $4.13 billion in global production and sustainment contracts through the F-35 program to date." Since the writing of Trantner's piece, during Israel's active genocide in Gaza, the Australian Army has drawn controversy by awarding a billion-dollar contract to Israeli arms manufacturer Elbit Systems.

As we've discussed many times, Australia is functionally a military and intelligence asset of the same US-centralized empire as Israel. We're currently falling all over ourselves helping the US prepare for a future war with China, and we've been providing logistical support for the US and UK bombing campaign against Ansarallah in Yemen. If all the violence and chaos we're seeing in the middle east leads to the US committing to a direct full-scale war in the region, we may be absolutely certain that Canberra will march us into that one as well. All while the empire cages an Australian journalist in a maximum security prison for exposing its war crimes.

Australia, like Israel, is not a real country. Like Israel, Australia is nothing other than a settler-colonialist outpost of western imperialism built on genocide, ethnic cleansing and theft, and now operates in a way that is inseparable from the US war machine. This land will never know peace or justice until we have extricated ourselves from the talons of the empire.

Featured image via Adobe Stock.

Idiot Republicans Are Saying Genocide Joe Has 'Abandoned Israel'

Dopey Republican pundits and politicians have begun claiming that Joe Biden has "abandoned Israel" and has fallen under the control of Hamas, because this is a presidential election year and everything needs to be ten times dumber than usual.

Read Let This Radicalize You
@JoshuaPHill · Follow

X

We've reached the moment you've all been waiting for: "Joe Biden is Hamas"

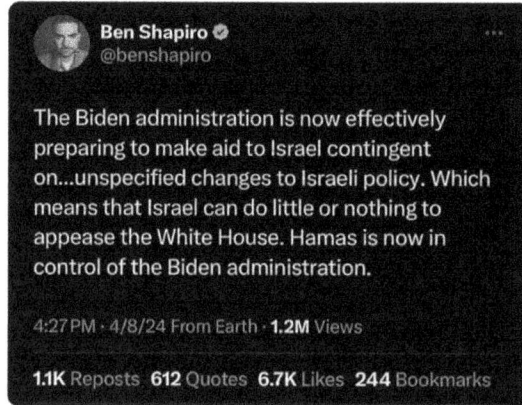

> **Ben Shapiro** ✓
> @benshapiro
>
> The Biden administration is now effectively preparing to make aid to Israel contingent on...unspecified changes to Israeli policy. Which means that Israel can do little or nothing to appease the White House. Hamas is now in control of the Biden administration.
>
> 4:27 PM · 4/8/24 From Earth · **1.2M** Views
>
> **1.1K** Reposts **612** Quotes **6.7K** Likes **244** Bookmarks

1:01 PM · Apr 9, 2024

♥ 11.1K   💬 Reply   🔗 Copy link

Read 100 replies

Donald Trump said on the campaign trail on Wednesday that "Any Jewish person that votes for a Democrat or votes for Biden should have their head examined," saying of Biden, "He totally abandoned Israel."

Trump's comments were made in response to Biden saying that Israel should declare a ceasefire of six to eight weeks, seemingly suggesting that Israel should do so without conditioning the ceasefire on the release of Israeli hostages. This hopeful statement was swiftly dispelled by Biden

himself, however, with the president reiterating the same keep-killing-children-until-Hamas-gives-us-everything-we-want position that this administration has stood by for six months. Apparently Biden's dementia-addled brain is just struggling to keep its story straight.

Meanwhile Daily Wire founder Ben Shapiro has been pushing the narrative that Biden has "saved" Hamas by capitulating to demands from the left on Gaza, going so far as to declare that "Hamas is now in control of the Biden administration."

To be clear, this is all foam-brained nonsense. Biden has spent six months pouring weapons of mass murder into Israel without any conditions whatsoever, and his administration has been justifying and spinning and making excuses for all of Israel's heinous actions in Gaza this entire time. No US president in history has done more to directly serve the murderousness of the Israeli war machine than Joe Biden.

Right to this very day the president is declaring "ironclad" support for Israel as fears mount that Iran may retaliate for the Israeli strike on its consulate building in Syria which killed multiple Iranian military officers, despite the fact that Iran has made it clear to the White House that if the US comes to Israel's defense it will make the US a target as well. Biden is so fanatically pro-Israel that we could be near

JUST IN: Trump Says 'Any Jewish Person That Votes For A Democrat'...
Forbes BREAKING NEWS
Watch on YouTube

the precipice of the worst-case nightmare scenario of all possible middle eastern conflicts because of his unwavering support for the genocidal apartheid state.

In reality, the only reason Republicans have begun trying to frame Biden as anti-Israel is because only through fiction and fantasy can America's two mainstream parties pretend there are any significant differences between them. They're both insanely supportive of Israel and its crimes. They both support war, militarism, imperialism, capitalism and oligarchy. The only areas in which there's any meaningful disagreement between them are the issues that don't inconvenience the powerful in any way like whether or not you're allowed to have an abortion or whether it's good or bad to be mean to trans people—and even those issues are only used to keep everyone's interest and attention locked into mainstream politics and diverted from revolutionary sentiment.

So they make up these moronic fictional battlegrounds to fight on, because that's the only way they can actually have anything to fight about. Joe Biden is a Hamas agent. Donald Trump is a Kremlin agent. Joe Biden is controlled by "the CCP". Donald Trump is going to be another Hitler instead of another shitty Republican. The Democrats want to steal your guns and make your son wear a dress. The Republicans want to dismantle NATO and let Vladimir Putin take over the world.

Absolutely none of this is real, but if Republicans and Democrats were forced to campaign against each other solely on issues in which they truly disagreed, they'd have very little to talk about, and it would give the whole two-party scam away. Before you know it you'd have them arguing about things like whether it would be best to ramp up nuclear aggressions with China first or prioritize taking out Russia, and people would start to notice that neither of these parties have the interests of normal human beings at heart.

So they keep up their kayfabe combat schtick, and sell it as hard as they can to make sure as many Americans as possible are clapping along to the pretend drama of the two-handed puppet show.

Can't wait til this election is over and done with so we can go back to the normal levels of stupid.

Featured images via Wikimedia Commons.

CNN Finally Tells The Truth About The Flour Massacre After Previously Shilling For Israel

CNN has a new report out showing that (surprise!) Israel lied about the Flour Massacre in which IDF troops fired machine guns into a crowd of starving Gazans waiting for food this past February, killing over a hundred people. CNN found that Israel's timeline and version of events doesn't line up with video footage, witness testimony, and forensic evidence.

Which of course was obvious from the beginning to anyone who isn't deeply invested in pretending Israel ever tells the truth about these things. Within hours of the massacre Euro-Med Human Rights Monitor had a preliminary report up saying that video, audio and material evidence shows that the IDF had been firing into the crowd in contradiction of Israel's claims that the injuries and deaths sustained on the scene were mostly due to Gazans trampling on each other in a mad rush upon the convoy of aid trucks. Now here's CNN, a month and a half later, telling us essentially the same thing.

This is the same CNN who at the time reported on the Flour Massacre in ways that advanced Israel's information interests with headlines completely exonerating Israel of any wrongdoing like "At least 100 killed and 700 injured in chaotic incident" and "Carnage at Gaza food aid site amid Israeli gunfire". CNN also repeatedly refers to the killings as "food aid deaths", as though it's the food aid that killed them and not the military of a very specific state power.

I don't know if there's a word for when a government does something evil and then churns out a bunch of easily disprovable lies with the understanding that by the time those lies are debunked public attention will have moved on from the controversy, but there should be. Over and over again we've seen the Israeli regime do just enough lying to dampen the initial burst of attention and outrage and get people doubting themselves, only to discover far too late that it was all a bunch of crap after the initial crime has been forgotten.

Jason Hickel @jasonhickel

The @guardian is calling the massacre "food aid-related deaths". I cannot believe what I am seeing.

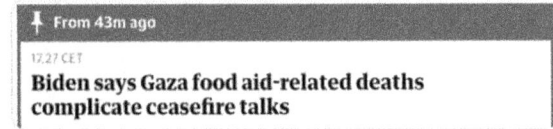

From 43m ago

17.27 CET

Biden says Gaza food aid-related deaths complicate ceasefire talks

4:12 AM · Mar 1, 2024 · 343.3K Views

3,061 Reposts 232 Quotes 8,650 Likes 279 Bookmarks

mike @__mike91 · Follow

in just 3 weeks, israel went from faking phone calls to say it never bombed a hospital to just bombing hospitals without a care in the world.

6:07 PM · Nov 8, 2023

51.1K Reply Copy link

Read 65 replies

Sana Saeed
@SanaSaeed

"Chaotic incident"?

The word you're looking for here, CNN, is massacre.

> **CNN Breaking News** @cnnbrk · 7h
>
> At least 100 killed and 700 injured in chaotic incident where IDF opened fire as people waited for food in Gaza, Palestinian officials say
> cnn.com/middleeast/liv...

12:12 AM · Mar 1, 2024 · **1.4M** Views

20.5K Reposts   **80** Quotes   **54.7K** Likes   **934** Bookmarks

This is exactly what happened with Israel's initial assault on al-Shifa Hospital back in November, when Israel was cranking out propaganda claiming the hospital was being used as a command center for Hamas. Not until the end of December did The Washington Post show up to acknowledge the abundantly obvious fact that there was no evidence for Israel's claims, which independent outlets like Consortium News had been reporting since mid-November. Now al-Shifa Hospital—the largest hospital in Gaza—has been completely destroyed.

Back in October Israel and its apologists were shrieking with outrage that anyone would dare suggest that Israel would ever attack a hospital at all, saturating the media with bogus evidence that it falsely claimed proved its innocence. Since that time Israel has launched hundreds of attacks on Gaza's healthcare services and has destroyed most of its healthcare system.

It's a weaponization of the adage "A lie gets halfway around the world before the truth even puts its boots on." They know all they have to do is lie really hard for a week or two, and then when the truth inevitably surfaces it won't matter, because the truth will never be able to have the impact their lies had when it mattered.

It's so obnoxious how even after all this time Israel is still given the benefit of the doubt on such claims by the western political-media class until they're debunked weeks or months later, long after the outcry over the incident has been muted and neutered by Israeli lies. If a state power is preventing journalists and human rights groups from investigating the facts on the ground in a given area, then it is not legitimate to give their claims about what happens in that area weighted consideration when their track record and all the facts in evidence say they're probably lying.

The fact that the western press keep giving Israel the benefit of the doubt whenever reports like this emerge after they've been caught in so very many lies means the western press are just as culpable for the circulation of Israeli lies as Israel itself. In journalism you're taught that if someone says it's raining and someone else says it's dry, your job isn't to quote them both and treat both claims as equal, your job is to go look out the window and see which is true. The fact that the imperial media take so long to drag their asses to the window serves nobody but Israel and the globe-spanning empire of which it is a part.

Featured image via Adobe Stock.

Mehdi Hasan ✓ 𝕏
@mehdirhasan · Follow

The Flour Massacre was indeed a flour massacre.

As I told @abbydphillip on CNN that night, we shouldn't trust the Israeli military's initial and kneejerk denials. They lie. They're good at lying.

And, now, CNN's own latest and important investigation proves me right:

> **Eliza Mackintosh** @elizamackintosh
>
> CNN's analysis of dozens of videos and testimonies from 22 eyewitnesses' casts doubt on the Israeli military's timeline of February 29, when more than 100 people were killed and 700 injured during a food aid delivery southwest of Gaza City.
> edition.cnn.com/2024/04/09/mid...

9:23 AM · Apr 10, 2024 ⓘ

♥ 6.3K   Reply   Copy link

Read 150 replies

Israeli Suffering Is Not Comparable To Palestinian Suffering

• Notes From The Edge Of The Narrative Matrix •

The mass media are once again pushing the narrative that Israel is "scaling back" its operations in Gaza, which as journalist Sana Saeed noted on Twitter is a claim they've been falsely making for months. To promote such stories even as Israel publicly declares that it's preparing for an invasion of Rafah is absurd and irresponsible.

•

A member of the Israeli Knesset named Limor Son Har-Melech says there are secret Israeli plans to establish settlements in the Gaza Strip. It sure is a crazy coincidence how every single part of Israel's response to October 7 has looked exactly the same as what it would look like if Israel just started doing all the things that it has wanted to do to the Palestinians for generations.

•

I'm sick of hearing October 7 mentioned in the same breath as Israel's incineration of Gaza as though they're equal or even comparable. A thousand Israelis dying (probably hundreds by indiscriminate IDF fire) is not comparable to tens of thousands of Palestinians (probably more) being deliberately exterminated by high tech war machinery, even if before you account for the fact that Israel was the aggressor and that the violence of the oppressed is not comparable to the violence of the oppressor in the first place.

But that's what you'll hear all the time from polite western liberals trying to walk a center line on the Israel-Palestine issue. They'll talk about how "sad" and "tragic" and "heartbreaking" BOTH the butchery in Gaza AND October 7 are, giving equal weight to two exponentially unequal acts of violence.

This is the same as lying. It actively misrepresents what's actually going on, leading to widespread misunderstanding like the fact that half of Americans have no idea whether more Palestinians or Israelis are being killed in the current "war". Trying to balance out two wildly unbalanced events gives people a wildly unbalanced understanding of what's really happening, leading to a wildly unbalanced worldview. But you see this constantly, and the western political-media class do everything they can to feed into it.

Israeli suffering is not equal to Palestinian suffering. It's not even in the same ballpark. Pretending otherwise is deceitful and manipulative.

•

Biden has declared "ironclad" support for Israel as fears mount that Iran will soon retaliate for the Israeli strike on its consulate building in Syria which killed multiple Iranian military officers, despite the fact that Iran has made it clear to the White House that if the US comes to Israel's defense it will make the US a target as well. We could be near the precipice of the worst-case nightmare scenario of all possible middle eastern conflicts because of this president's unwavering support for the genocidal Zionist state.

•

In the early weeks of Israel's assault Palestinian journalists were filling social media with footage of Israeli atrocities in Gaza. We're seeing far less footage now because the journalists have been killed and access to the internet made far more difficult and Palestinian access to much of Gaza has been restricted, but it's important to remember that those atrocities have continued to happen this entire time.

•

Normal person: It's bad to murder children
Crazy person: Aha I see you hate the Jewish faith

•

"It's so sad and tragic that children are being fed to the Child Incineration Machine," said the liberal while loading the children onto the conveyor belt. "It's heartbreaking!"

•

Is there a word for the tactic where a government does something evil and then throws out a bunch of flimsy lies right off the bat to mute the initial backlash, so when the truth comes out public attention has moved on and it has no impact? Whatever that is, Israel excels at it.

•

Funny how people get so emotionally invested in US presidential elections when the whole system's stacked to ensure that each party wins half the time. It's like putting 10 blue marbles and 10 red ones in a hat and crying when you pull out a red one and celebrating when it's blue.

Featured image via Wikimedia Commons.

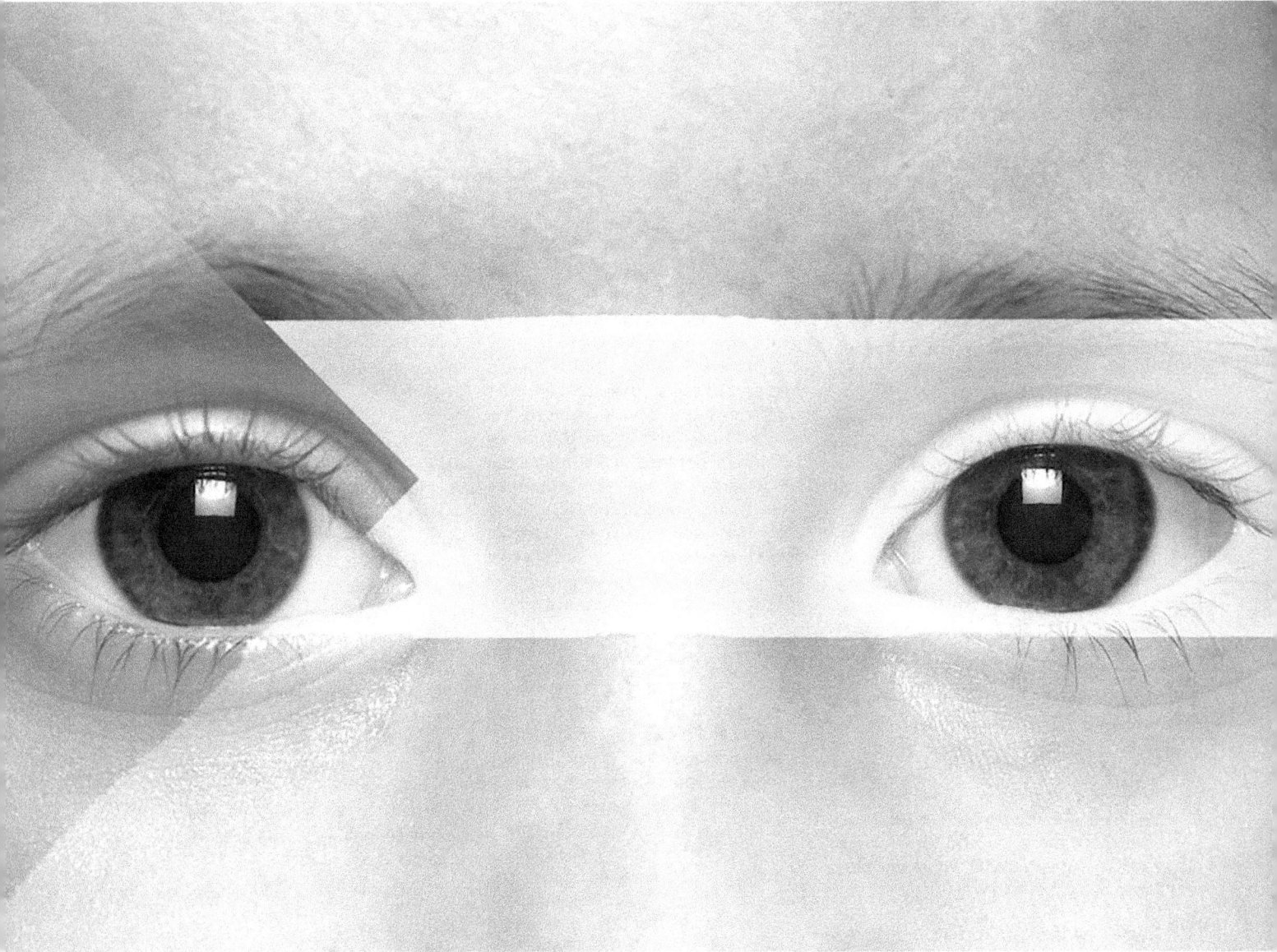

Getting Gaza Right Is The Absolute Bare Minimum Requirement

Gaza is simpler than Iraq. Iraq was simpler than Yemen. Yemen was simpler than Libya. Libya was simpler than Ukraine. Ukraine is simpler than Syria. Gaza is the simplest and most straightforward of all the evil interventions of the US murder machine in recent memory—which is why I've got no patience for anyone who gets it wrong.

I'm a lot more forgiving of people who bought into the imperial narrative about Syria and believed that country erupted in violence because Assad just went ape shit and started killing innocent people for no reason, because it takes a lot of work to sort out fact from fiction about what actually happened there. There were really good journalists who got Syria wrong at first in the early years of the conflict, just because there was so much information to comb through and so much aggressive imperial narrative management about it. There was so much less visibility into the facts on the ground in Syria than there is in Gaza, and there were so many complex narrative control ops muddying the waters.

Gaza isn't like that. What's happening really could not be more obvious. A nuclear-armed high tech military has been raining bombs and inflicting siege warfare upon a densely packed, walled-in civilian population, half of whom are children, with the full backing of the most powerful empire that has ever existed. We've been seeing a constant stream of footage showing children ripped apart by military explosives and starved to skeletons, Israeli soldiers posting videos of themselves gleefully doing some of the most sadistic and depraved things you can imagine, destroyed hospitals, carpet-bombed neighborhoods, and Israelis blocking aid trucks from feeding starving people.

This is not the slightest bit complicated. It's as subtle as a kick in the teeth. There is no excuse for getting this one wrong now. There's not even any excuse for getting it wrong on day one. It's been obvious this entire time. Any politician, pundit or journalist who's gotten it wrong can be dismissed as completely worthless, even if they're beginning to come around now after they sensed the wind blowing against Israel in recent weeks.

Gaza is a test of the absolute bare minimum requirements for someone to be worth listening to about anything at all, because if you got this one wrong then there's just something wrong with you as a human being. You're too fucked up and twisted inside to have a clear vision into anything that's happening in the world. You're not in touch with your own humanity enough to have any useful insight into humanity as a collective. You have wasted your time on this planet. You've managed to spend your entire life without learning any of the more meaningful lessons that can be learned here.

And there are plenty of people getting Gaza right who are buying into all kinds of other imperial propaganda spin about other international affairs and conflicts, which is to be expected—being able to understand the simplest possible foreign policy issue doesn't mean you'll be able to grasp the more complicated ones. But every one of them stands head and shoulders above everyone who couldn't see the destruction of Gaza for what it is. They might fail other tests, but at least they passed the first one.

Everything I'm saying here will all be completely obvious to everyone one day. People will look back on what was done to Gaza and struggle to comprehend how the world could have allowed such a thing when it was all happening right out in the open for everybody to see. And if I'm still around I will struggle to explain it myself, because it baffles me here and now in the present moment. It probably always will.

Featured image via Adobe Stock.

Empire Managers Keep Acting Like Iran Is About To Attack Israel Without Provocation

[DATELINE: APR 13, 2024]

Iran appears to be poised to launch an attack on Israel in retaliation for the Israeli strike on an Iranian consulate building adjacent to the Iranian embassy in Damascus, which killed 16 people including multiple Iranian military officers. Iranian forces have already seized an Israeli-linked cargo ship in the Strait of Hormuz, and Tehran continues to vow that it will soon retaliate for the embassy attack at an undisclosed time.

Iran has reportedly said through Oman that the scope of the attack will be calibrated to avoid escalation into an all-out regional conflict. Reuters reports that Washington does not expect the retaliatory attack to be large enough to draw the US into war, so both Washington and Tehran appear to be saying basically the same thing about what's coming. So as things stand right now it seems both sides see it as unlikely that this will be the spark to ignite a new war of profound horror in the middle east.

What's really interesting about this situation right now is how western empire managers and propagandists have been framing the coming Iranian retaliation to suggest that Iran is about to attack Israel out of the blue, completely unprovoked. As though bombing an embassy would not be considered an extreme act of war by any nation anywhere on earth.

They've seriously just been talking about it as though the embassy strike didn't happen, babbling about defending Israel and Israel's right to defend itself like any attack by Iran would be coming completely out of the blue. On Friday President Biden warned Iran not to attack Israel when questioned about the coming strike, saying, "We are devoted to the defense of Israel. We will support Israel. We will help defend Israel and Iran will not succeed."

"The threats from Iran are completely unacceptable and we, like the Americans, fully support Israel's right to defend itself," said British Prime Minister Rishi Sunak on Thursday.

"Australia is deeply concerned by indications Iran is preparing military action against Israel," chimed in Australian Foreign Minister Penny Wong, saying Iran should "use its influence in the region to promote stability, not contribute to escalation."

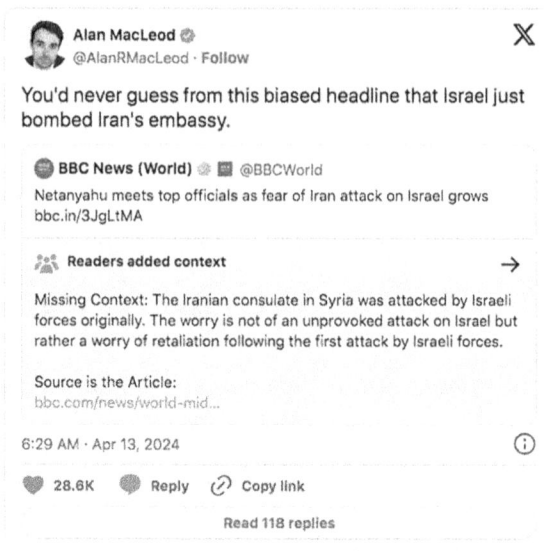

"Israel is under threat of imminent attack by Iran," said US Senator Tom Cotton on Twitter. "President Biden needs to warn the ayatollahs immediately that the United States will back Israel to the hilt and the joint American-Israeli retaliation for any attack will be swift and devastating."

"Iran will bear the consequences for choosing to escalate the situation any further," IDF spokesman Daniel Hagari said following the cargo ship seizure.

Mass media headlines have also been framing this as an attack that's coming completely out of nowhere by an irrational aggressor.

"Netanyahu meets top officials as fear of Iran attack on Israel grows," reads a headline from the BBC.

"Israel braces amid fears of Iranian strike; U.S. shifts forces to region," a headline from The Washington Post says.

"Israel Bracing for Unprecedented Direct Iran Attack in Days," blares Bloomberg.

"Major Iranian attack on Israel believed to be imminent," warns CBS News.

The casual news consumer would see all this and assume that Israel and its allies have received some intelligence that Iran is preparing an attack without provocation, and are doing everything they can to deter this maniacal regime from doing so.

This is ridiculous. If Iran had bombed a US embassy and killed multiple US military officials, the US would be raining bombs on Tehran within hours and everyone knows it. But Israel bombs an Iranian embassy and everyone acts like it didn't happen and starts yelling at Iran instead.

It's like if someone ran up and sucker-punched somebody at the bar, and then everyone started screaming at the guy who just got punched that he'd better leave the other guy alone and stop being a bully.

Iran is probably going to attack Israel, because at some point it does have to push back on Israeli violence to create some deterrence. Hopefully it will indeed be limited, hopefully the violence will not spiral into something nightmarish, and hopefully enough people are able to see through all the propaganda spin enough to understand what's actually happening.

Featured image via Rawpixel.

US Declines Israel's Invitation To Start WW3 [For Now]

[DATELINE: APR 14, 2024]

Iran has carried out its long-promised retaliation for Israel's attack on its consulate building in Damascus, launching a massive barrage of drones and missiles which it claims hit and destroyed Israeli military targets, while Israel says they dealt only superficial damage with a few injuries. The US and its allies reportedly helped shoot down a number of the Iranian projectiles.

Just as we discussed in the lead-up to the strike, the western political-media class are acting as though this was a completely unprovoked attack launched against the innocent, Bambi-eyed victim Israel. Comments from western officials and pundits and headlines from the mass media are omitting the fact that Israel instigated these hostilities with its extreme act of aggression in Syria as much as possible. Here in Australia the Sydney Morning Herald write-up about the strike didn't get around to informing its readers about the attack on the Iranian consulate until the tenth paragraph of the article, and said only that Iran had "accused" Israel of launching the attack because Israel has never officially confirmed it.

In any case, Iran says the attack is now over. Given that we're not seeing any signs of massive damage, Iran's reported claim that its retaliation would be calibrated to avoid escalation into a full-scale regional war seems to have been accurate, as does Washington's reported claim that it didn't expect the strike to be large enough to draw the US into war.

A new report from Axios says Biden has personally told Netanyahu that the US will not be supporting any Israeli military response to the Iranian strike. An anonymous senior White House official told Axios that Biden said to Netanyahu, "You got a win. Take the win," in reference to the number of Iranian weapons that were taken out of the sky by the international coalition in Israel's defense. Apparently helping to mitigate the damage from the Iranian attack is all the military commitment the White House is willing to make against Iran at this time.

And thank all that is holy for that. A war between the US alliance and Iran and its allies would be the stuff of nightmares, making the horrors we've been seeing in Gaza these last six months look like an episode of Peppa Pig.

Robert Wright
@robertwrighter · Follow

Read this piece on why Bibi chose to radically escalate with his April 1 strike on Iran's diplomatic compound. It's by Paul Pillar, who knows the territory--he was once in charge of analysis of the Middle East for CIA & all other US intelligence agencies.

responsiblestatecraft.org
Is Israel's plan to draw the US into a war with Iran?
Netanyahu must know Tehran will respond militarily to the attack on its embassy in Syria, the question is whether American troops will be a ...

7:59 AM · Apr 14, 2024

❤ 326   💬 Reply   🔗 Copy link

Read 15 replies

But Washington merely declining to get involved is nowhere near enough. As the Quincy Institute's Trita Parsi quipped on Twitter, "Biden needs to PREVENT further escalation, not just declare his desire to stay out of it."

Indeed, Israel has already made it clear that it is going to be moving forward with an escalation against Iran. Israel's Channel 12 cites an unnamed senior official saying the Iranian counter strike is going to receive an "unprecedented response".

Trita Parsi ✓
@tparsi · Follow

Not significant enough.

Biden needs to PREVENT further escalation, not just declare his desire to stay out of it.

🧑 **Jim Sciutto** ✓ @jimsciutto
This is significant:

Biden made clear to Netanyahu that the US will not participate in any offensive operations against Iran, @mj_lee to me on the air just now.

1:40 PM · Apr 14, 2024

❤ 1K   💬 Reply   🔗 Copy link

Read 49 replies

"Israel has already informed the Americans and governments in the region that its response is inevitable," The Economist reports. "Its military options include launching drones at Iran, and long-range airstrikes on Iran, possibly on military bases or nuclear installations."

It's unclear at this time how much the latest message from the Biden administration will affect the calculations of this position, but the mass media are reporting that White House officials are worried Israel is getting ready to do something extremely reckless that could draw the US into a war it would rather avoid.

NBC News reports the following:

"Some top U.S. officials are concerned Israel could do something quickly in response to Iran's attacks without thinking through potential fallout afterward, according to a senior administration official and a senior defense official.

"Those concerns stem in part from the administration's views of the approach Israel has taken to its war against Hamas, as well as the attack in Damascus.

"President Joe Biden has privately expressed concern that Israeli Prime Minister Benjamin Netanyahu is trying to drag the U.S. more deeply into a broader conflict, according to three people familiar with his comments."

People have been raising this concern for some time now. Earlier this month Responsible Statecraft's Paul Pillar wrote up a solid argument that Netanyahu stands a lot to gain personally from drawing the US into a war with Iran to help him with his legal and political troubles and take the focus off of Israel's genocide in Gaza.

Whether that's the case or not it's pretty absurd for the Biden administration to just sit around passively hoping this doesn't happen as though it wouldn't have a say in the matter, and as though there's nothing it can do to prevent such an occurrence right now. Biden has had the ability to end this insane cycle of escalation in the middle east since it started six months ago by demanding a ceasefire in Gaza and demanding that Israel rein in its murder machine, just as US presidents have done successfully in the past.

Biden could end all this with one phone call. The fact that he doesn't means he's a monster, and no amount of mass media reports about how "concerned" and "frustrated" he is regarding Israel's actions will ever change that.

Featured image via Adobe Stock.

Anyone Who Wants The US To Attack Iran Is An Enemy Of Humanity
• Notes From The Edge Of The Narrative Matrix •

Anyone who wants the US and its allies to attack Iran is a psychopath. People who want to unleash a war of that scale upon our species should be rejected from our society as aggressively as child molesters and Nazis.

•

The Spectator Index ✓
@spectatorindex · Follow

X

BREAKING: NBC News reports that 'President Joe Biden has privately expressed concern that Israeli Prime Minister Benjamin Netanyahu is trying to drag the U.S. more deeply into a broader conflict'

12:06 PM · Apr 14, 2024

ⓘ

💜 18.2K   💬 Reply   🔗 Copy link

Read 924 replies

A new CNN report says multiple Biden administration officials "saw Iran's attacks on Israel Saturday as disproportionate to Israel's strikes in Damascus that prompted the retaliation."

There are zero reported fatalities as a result of the Iranian retaliation. The Israeli strikes on the Iranian embassy in Damascus killed 16 people, including multiple high-level Iranian military officials. To see Iran's response as "disproportionate" is to admit you believe Israeli lives are worth literally orders of magnitude more than Iranian lives.

And it was at an embassy, for god's sake. Israel can assassinate 16 people while shattering decades of diplomatic norms, and in the eyes of the US that's still not as bad as Iran creating a few potholes in an Israeli street.

And anyway how obscene is it that these shitstains can babble about proportionality at all after backing Israel's mass atrocities in Gaza? When Iran attacks the response needs to be proportionate, but when Israel incinerates Gaza over October 7 it's "LMAO fuck around and find out, laughcry emoji, Israeli flag."

•

After six months of mass murder and chaos the only thing that looks more absurd than the claim that Israel is morally superior to other nations in the middle east is the claim that the United States is morally superior to other nations in the world.

No matter how low your opinion was of western power structures and western civilization, if you've been watching events of the last six months with sincerity it will have sunk even lower by now.

•

It's so obnoxious how the mass media are helping the White House pretend this is something the Biden administration is just passively sitting around hoping doesn't happen, as though the US hasn't had the power to end all this every single day for the last six months.

•

It's just an easily quantifiable fact that the Trump administration was vastly less warlike and murderous than the Biden administration has been. This doesn't mean Trump wasn't warlike and murderous. It doesn't even mean Trump wouldn't have been doing more or less the same evil things that Biden has been doing if he'd won in 2020. But it does mean the entire mainstream liberal narrative about what Trump is and what Biden is has been complete bullshit this entire time, which necessarily means the whole mainstream narrative about the US political system is a lie.

•

Caitlin Johnstone ✔
@caitoz · Follow

X

No no you don't understand, this time Germany is rounding up Jews to FIGHT antisemitism.

Ali Abunimah ✔ @AliAbunimah · ✏

Video I just received shows @PolizeiBerlin_l arresting the spokesperson of Jewish Voice for Peace in Germany, Udi Raz, as horrified onlookers shout "Never Again!" amid these scenes so reminiscent of Germany's Nazi past (present) #PalaestinaKongress

7:38 AM · Apr 13, 2024

♥ 9K   Reply   Copy link

Read 63 replies

•

It's possible that as the United States was first beginning to move toward planetary hegemony there were some empire managers operating in good faith who sincerely believed US unipolarity could be a force for achieving world peace. It's doubtful that everyone constructing this monstrosity has been an evil, mustache-twirling cartoon villain who wanted to see nonstop violence, oppression and nuclear brinkmanship inflicted upon populations around the globe. But that's what wound up happening.

And of course it did. The belief that a regime can take over the world by any amount of force necessary and create peace and prosperity for all was always a poorly reasoned fantasy of deeply unwise minds. Of course there are going to be populations who refuse to be subjugated, and some of them are going to have nuclear weapons, and others will have conventional weapons but defend their sovereignty tooth and claw. Most of the violence and cold war brinkmanship you see in international conflicts today is a direct result of this dynamic.

The US-centralized empire's foreign policy is one long and unrelenting war against disobedience. It simply is not possible to bring the entire human species under one single power umbrella without copious amounts of violence and tyranny. If we keep going along this trajectory, the empire's war on disobedience is going to lead to nuclear armageddon someday.

Featured image via Gage Skidmore (CC BY-SA 2.0 DEED)

Israel's Latest Lie Is That It Has 'No Choice' But To Attack Iran

[DATELINE: APR 16, 2024]

In an article titled "Israel vows to retaliate against Iran for missile attacks," Axios reports that the Israeli defense minister has informed his American counterpart that Israel "has no choice" but to attack Iran for the retaliatory strike it launched in response to Israel's deadly attack on the Iranian embassy in Damascus.

"Israeli Minister of Defense Yoav Gallant told Defense Secretary Lloyd Austin Sunday that Israel has no choice but to respond to the unprecedented missile and drone attack launched by Iran over the weekend," reports Axios, citing an anonymous US official and another unnamed source.

The state of Israel has been churning out massive lies on a daily basis for the last six months, but this whopper could wind up being the most consequential.

Obviously Israel has a choice as to whether it continues to escalate a conflict it initiated with an extreme act of aggression. This fraudulent apartheid ethnostate is so accustomed to crying victim every minute of every day that it will even pretend to be the victim of its own conscious decisions.

As professor Jason Hickel put it on Twitter, "People need to understand that Israel*does not*need to retaliate. Iran's action was a telegraphed response to Israel's bombing of its consulate, which killed 16 people and violated the Vienna Convention. Iran says they now consider the matter closed. Israel must de-escalate."

> **Trita Parsi** ✓ X
> @tparsi · Follow
>
> My latest for @ForeignPolicy on Iran, Gaza & Israel:
>
> Biden's support for Israel is often described as a continuation of a long-standing US policy. In reality, it is a break with tradition. Previous presidents regularly twisted Israel's arm if needed.
>
>
> foreignpolicy.com
> Netanyahu Wants War With Iran. Biden Can Prevent It.
> Past U.S. presidents rejected Israel's push to strike Tehran, but Biden is falling into his trap.
>
> 3:40 AM · Apr 16, 2024 ⓘ
>
> 🤍 481   Reply   Copy link
>
> Read 36 replies

> **Abas Aslani** X
> @AbasAslani · Follow
>
> Iranian DepFM Ali Bagheri says that #Iran will respond to a new mistake by #Israel "in seconds, not in days or hours". He said, "This time, they will not have 12 days".
>
> ○ **Iran Nuances** @IranNuances
> #Iran's deputy foreign minister Ali Bagheri: Israeli regime needs to know that in case of another mistake they will not have 12 days and the response will be given in seconds not in days or hours. #Israel
>
>
> 5:55 AM · Apr 16, 2024 ⓘ
>
> 🤍 140   Reply   Copy link
>
> Read 6 replies

Iran's deputy foreign minister Ali Bagheri has made it clear that if Israel launches another attack against Iran, this time Iran's response will be instantaneous instead of a twelve-day grace period with Tehran giving neighboring countries and the United States a 72-hour advance warning to ensure minimal damage to Israel.

Predictably, the Biden administration is doing its usual phony schtick where it pretends to be a passive witness to all this, with National Security spokesman John Kirby telling the press that the White House plans to just "wait and see what the Israelis decide to do."

Report: Israel Tells US It Has No Choice But To Respond to Iran
Israeli TV reports that Israel's War Cabinet has decided it will attack Iran, but it's unclear how or when
by Dave DeCamp
@DecampDave #Israel #Iran #Gaza
news.antiwar.com/2024/04/15/rep... Show more

4:16 AM · Apr 16, 2024

❤ 44   💬 Reply   🔗 Copy link

Read 9 replies

But as foreign policy analyst Tariq Kenney-Shawa noted of Kirby's statement, "Israel will be using US-supplied weapons, will have to coordinate with US forces throughout the region, and will depend on the US for missile defense when Iran responds." So the fact that the US won't be actively planning the attack with Israel doesn't mean the US won't be involved in it on a fundamental level.

If Israel's escalatory attack happens, it will be because Washington allowed it to. If the US informed Israel that it will instantly lose its pricey US weapons supplies and Pentagon support if it attacks Iran, Israel would discover very quickly that it does in fact have a choice as to whether or not to proceed.

In an article for Foreign Policy titled "Netanyahu Wants War With Iran. Biden Can Prevent It.", Quincy Institute's Trita Parsi argues that while Biden's unconditional support for Israel is often described as a continuation of longstanding US policy, it has actually been a rather dramatic break from the norm. Presidents like Reagan, both Bushes, and Obama have not hesitated to give Israel's arm a twist whenever they found it necessary to advance US interests in the region; this new policy of just letting Tel Aviv do whatever it wants while providing unconditional support is actually without precedent in the White House.

Both Israel and the US are pretending to be powerless in this situation, when in reality they're both anything but. They're like two muggers getting ready to mug someone and saying "If only there was something we could do to stop this terrible mugging!"

Israel absolutely can choose not to accelerate toward a terrifying war between extremely powerful militaries, and the US absolutely can choose to pump the brakes. The fact that neither of them are doing so is just what it looks like when you live under a globe-spanning empire that is fueled by human blood.

Featured image via Adobe Stock.

Stop Pretending Biden Is Some Passive Witness To Israel's Warmongering

The more I think about it the more obnoxious I find the Biden administration's "Gee whiz, I sure hope Israel doesn't drag us into a giant war in the middle east" posturing and the imperial media's facilitation of it.

CNN has a new article out titled "As Iran attacks Israel, Biden confronts an escalating Middle East crisis he had hoped to avoid," which is a genre of story that has been coming out in slightly different iterations again and again for the past six months. Every time Israel does something that makes things more dangerous in the middle east with the assistance of the United States, the American press fall all over themselves to inform the world that the president really doesn't want this to happen and that his feelings are very upset about it.

"For President Joe Biden, an attack on Israel launched from Iranian soil amounts to a scenario he'd greatly sought to avoid since the start of the current Middle East conflict," writes CNN, saying the strikes "heighten the risk of a wider regional conflict that could directly draw in the United States, along with other countries."

Assal Rad
@AssalRad · Follow
X

-Iran was *responding* to Israel's attack on its embassy, this framing makes it seem like Iran initiated an attack

-If Biden wanted to avoid a crisis he could have supported a ceasefire, instead he gave Israel no red line, aided atrocities in Gaza and shattered international law

CNN Politics   Live TV

After   response to   attack
As Iran ~~attacks~~ Israel~~'s~~ Biden confronts an escalating Middle East crisis he ~~had hoped to avoid~~ helped to create

By Kevin Liptak and MJ Lee, CNN

⏱ 5 minute read

Updated 8:18 AM EDT, Sun April 14, 2024

2:16 AM · Apr 15, 2024   ⓘ

♥ 9.5K   💬 Reply   🔗 Copy link

Read 168 replies

Megan K. Stack
@Megankstack · Follow
X

This administration's many leaks to the press about Israel always manage to make it sound like Biden is being held against his will and blinking twice to signal he needs help

IRAN TENSIONS

Biden officials worry that Israeli response to Iran's attack may trigger wider war

President Joe Biden has privately expressed concern that Israeli Prime Minister Benjamin Netanyahu is trying to drag Washington into a broader conflict, according to three people familiar with his comments.

3:40 AM · Apr 15, 2024   ⓘ

♥ 269   💬 Reply   🔗 Copy link

Read 16 replies

"Israel will respond to Iran's attack, but the scope of that response has yet to be determined," CNN reports, citing an anonymous Israeli official.

And it's just such an obscene insult to our intelligence to suggest that the Biden administration is some kind of passive witness to all this, sitting around wringing its hands hoping Israel doesn't do something so horrible that the United States will have no choice but to leap into World War Three in defense of its dear ally. It's insulting in that it asks us to believe the US would have no choice but to enter into a war of unimaginable horror if Israel acts belligerently enough, and it's insulting in that it asks us to ignore the fact that Biden could have ended this insane cycle of escalation with one phone call to Israel at any time over the last six months.

Being asked to accept that the Biden administration is just standing there hoping Israel doesn't ignite the worst war in middle eastern history is like seeing a dog owner letting their rottweiler run around biting people all over the neighborhood and saying "Yeah he just does what he likes, I just hope he doesn't kill anybody."

It's like, no. Stop that. You're not just crossing your fingers and hoping Israel doesn't do something monstrous, you're letting them do whatever they want because that's what you're choosing to do. Israel's entire existence is as dependent on US support as a scuba diver is on their oxygen tank, and as such the White House has essentially limitless leverage it can use to make Israel do as it pleases—and it has done so in the past. Hell it's done so during this very Gaza assault, successfully commanding Israel to stop cutting off Gazan telecommunications and to start letting more aid trucks in to the enclave.

If Biden truly didn't want Israel to be turning the middle east into a hurricane of death and fire, he would stop it. He would put the damn dog on a leash.

The western press have a well-established track record of consistently framing US wars as these traps that Washington just clumsily stumbles its way into, like there's some giant Macaulay Culkin-like deity sneaking around laying tripwires to force the Pentagon to regime change Libya or whatever. After a certain number of wars you have to figure that a regime is starting a bunch of wars because it's just a warmongering regime, though—and the US has been involved in a whole, whole lot of wars. Nobody's that clumsy or that unlucky; it's like believing your husband when he tells you he keeps slipping and falling with his man parts inside the lady parts of various coworkers.

The most powerful empire that has ever existed is not just passively sitting there praying that big bad Israel doesn't force it to go to war with Iran. That is not happening. All the violence and chaos that's happening in the middle east right now is happening because the US empire wants it to happen, and because the people who steer that empire are psychopathic ghouls. And don't let the crooked manipulators of the western mass media tell you otherwise.

Feature image official White House photo (public domain).

Assange Extradition Case Moves Forward While The CIA Covers Its Tracks

At the same time, CIA Director William Burns has filed a State Secrets Privilege demand to withhold information in a lawsuit against the agency by four American journalists and attorneys who were spied on during their visits to Assange at the Ecuadorian embassy in London. State secrets privilege is a US evidentiary rule designed to prevent courts from revealing state secrets during civil litigation; the CIA began invoking it with the Assange lawsuit earlier this year.

Burns argues:

> "I am asserting the state secrets and statutory privileges in this case as I have determined that either admitting or denying that CIA has information implicated by the remaining allegations in the Amended Complaint reasonably could be expected to cause serious—and in some cases, exceptionally grave—damage to the national security of the United States. After deliberation and personal consideration, I have determined that the complete factual bases for my privilege assertions cannot be set forth on the public record without confirming or denying whether CIA has information relating to this matter and therefore risking the very harm to U.S. national security that I seek to protect."

Which is obviously a load of horse shit. As Assange himself tweeted in 2017, "The overwhelming majority of information is classified to protect political security, not national security." Burns isn't worried about damaging "the national security of the United States," he's worried about the potential political fallout from information about the CIA spying on American lawyers and journalists while visiting a journalist who was being actively targeted by the legal arm of the US government.

Political security is also why the US is working to punish Julian Assange for publishing inconvenient facts about US war crimes. The Pentagon already acknowledged years ago that the Chelsea Manning leaks for which Assange is being prosecuted didn't get anyone killed and had no strategic impact on US war efforts, so plainly this isn't about national security. It's just politically damaging for the criminality of the US government to be made public for all to see.

They're just squeezing and squeezing this man as hard as they can for as long as they can get away with to keep him silent and make an example of him to show what happens when journalists reveal unauthorized information about the empire. Just like Gaza, the persecution of Julian Assange makes a lie of everything the US and its western allies claim to stand for, and reveals the cruel face of tyranny beneath the mask of liberal democracy.

Featured image via Adobe Stock.

Escalation With Iran Seemingly Over; Now We Have To Worry About Rafah

[DATELINE: APR 19, 2024]

The imperial media are reporting that Israel launched a missile attack against Iran early Friday morning, with explosions also seen in Syria and Iraq. Tehran is denying there was any missile attack on Iran at all, with Iranian media reporting that the blasts were actually from drones that were successfully shot down over Iran. It doesn't appear that any nuclear sites were struck.

Matthew Petti
@matthew_petti · Follow

X

Egyptian sources to The New Arab: "the US has accepted Israel's plan for an operation in the southern Gaza city of Rafah, in return for not carrying out a large strike in Iran in response to Tehran's unprecedented missile and drone attack."

timesofisrael.com
US agreed to Israel's plan for Rafah in return for not carrying out large...
• • •

4:35 PM · Apr 18, 2024

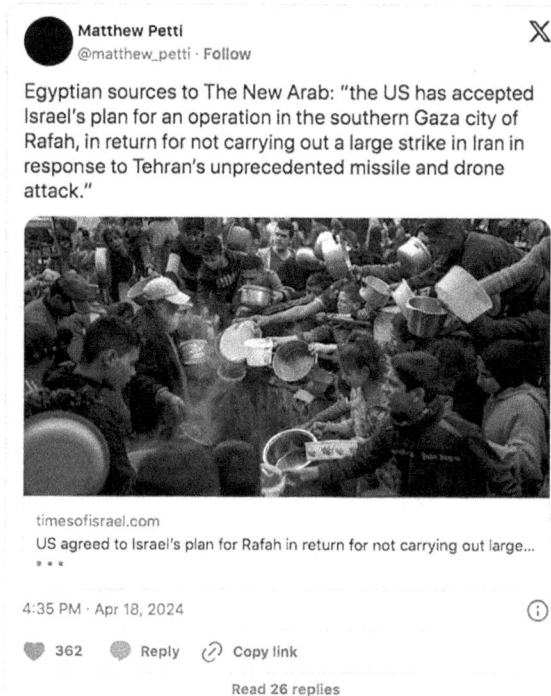

A senior Iranian official has reportedly told Reuters that Iran has no plans for any immediate response to Israel, which is good because Tehran has previously stated that if Israel makes another "mistake" it will result in immediate retaliation. Israel's extremist national security minister Itamar Ben-Gvir tweeted a word in Hebrew which roughly translates to "feeble" in an apparent reference to the Israeli attack, signaling his disapproval at Israel's failure to ignite World War Three.

So as things stand right now it looks like the cycle of escalation between Iran and Israel has thankfully ended or at least paused, which means now all we have to worry about is a horrific massacre in southern Gaza. The Times of Israel reports that Washington has agreed to go along with Israel's planned assault on the city of Rafah so long as Israel doesn't launch a large attack against Iran in response to its unprecedented retaliatory drone and missile attack on Saturday, according to an Egyptian source speaking to a Qatari outlet. A White House spokesperson has denied this, but you'd expect them to.

Israel had reportedly notified the US earlier on Thursday that an attack on Iran was coming, and that nuclear sites would not be damaged. If all Israel did was launch a small attack on Iran that did no significant damage, that would certainly fit the bill for the kind of strike that was alleged by the aforementioned Egyptian source.

As Dr Assal Rad said on Twitter regarding this report, "If this is true, Biden is green lighting a massacre so that Israel doesn't start a wider war with Iran."

Iran's retaliatory strike for Israel's attack on the Iranian consulate in Damascus reportedly delayed Israel's planned assault on Rafah, where according to CNN the IDF was ready to begin dropping leaflets on Monday. Israel has spent the last six months kettling the population of the Gaza Strip southward into Rafah, so now it's extremely densely populated and a full-on attack could be deadlier than anything we've seen in Gaza so far.

Featured image via Adobe Stock.

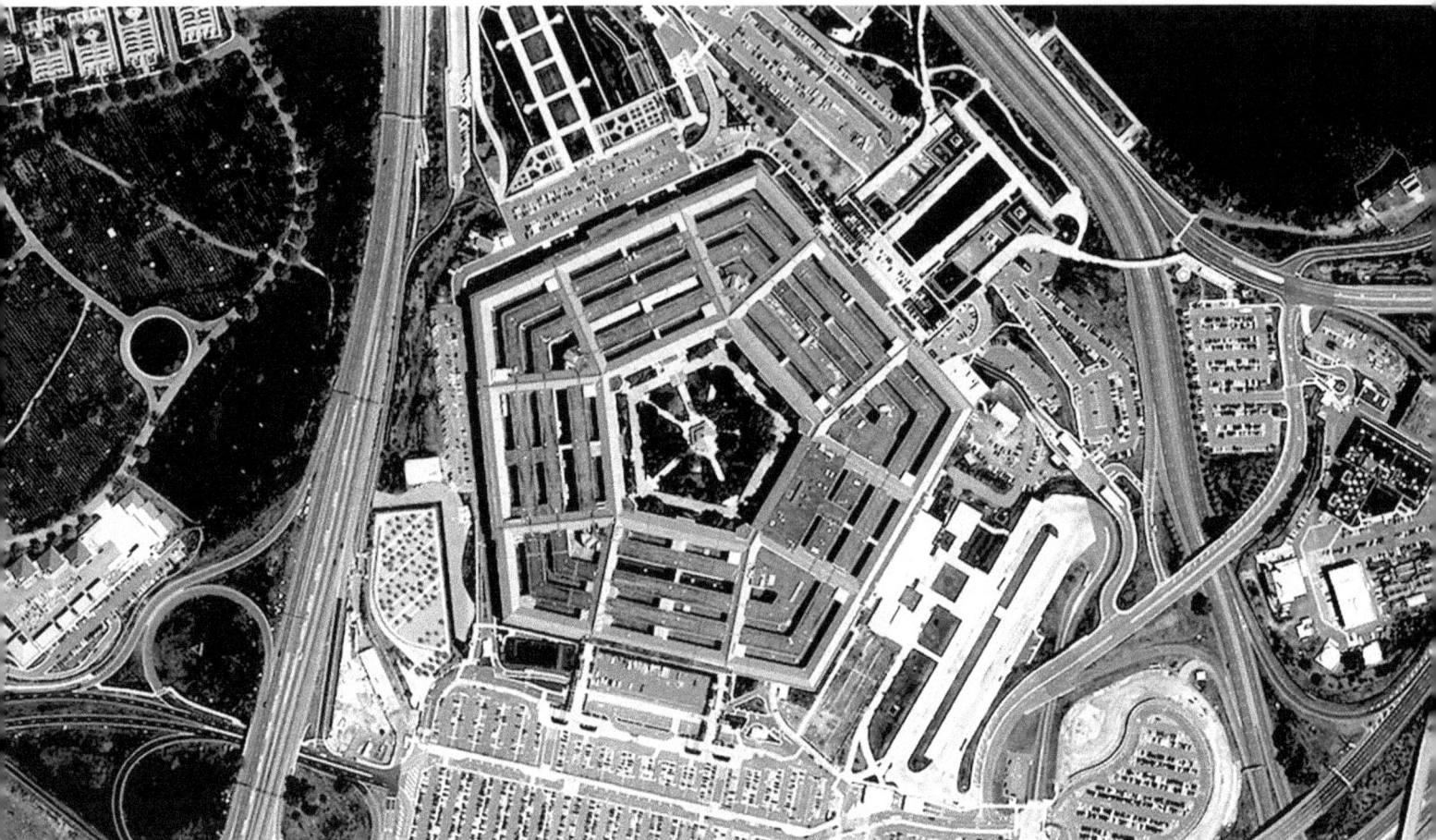

"Rules–Based Order" Means Rules For Thee But Not For We
• Notes From The Edge Of The Narrative Matrix •

Israel's allowed to bomb an Iranian consulate, but Iran's not allowed to strike back. The US is allowed to surround China with war machinery, but it would be World War Three if China ever tried to militarily encircle the US. NATO is allowed to expand to Russia's doorstep and amass proxy forces on its border, but the last time Moscow placed a credible military threat anywhere near the United States, the US responded so aggressively that the world almost ended.

The "rules-based international order" that the US-centralized power structure purports to uphold just means an order in which the US makes up the rules and nations had better obey them. It means rules for thee but not for me.

•

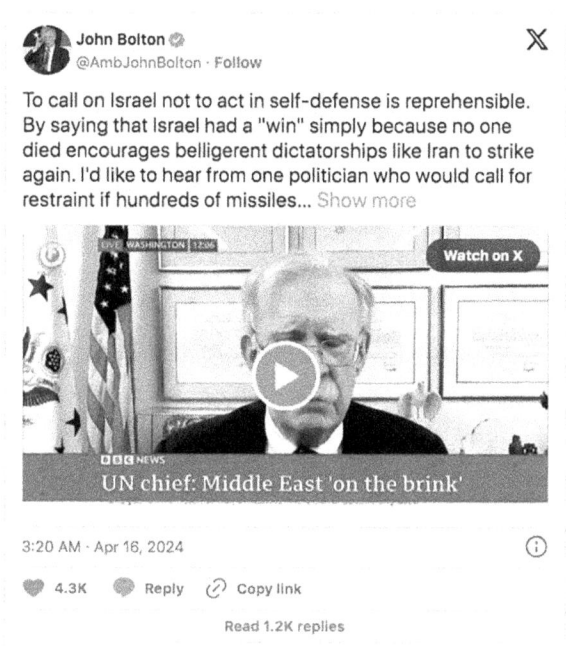

Democrats are currently committing genocide, pushing through terrifying NSA surveillance powers, and working to imprison a journalist for life for telling the truth about US war crimes, but it's very important to support Biden because if Trump wins, fascism might come to America.

•

The Assange extradition case is like if the mafia was demanding a snitch be extradited to Italy and multiple nations collaborated with them to help make this happen, except in this case the snitch is a journalist who told the truth, and the mob happens to run a global superpower.

•

The imperial media are once again trotting out John Bolton to help sell the idea of war with Iran. This monster belongs in a cage, not on camera. The fact that the mainstream western press keep having this completely discredited bloodthirsty psychopath on their shows to advocate every possible US war proves that our entire civilization is diseased.

•

Israel's actions over the last six months have made it abundantly clear that Biden's stated goal of preventing the outbreak of more war in the middle east and his stated "ironclad" support for Israel are two mutually exclusive positions. You can do one or the other, but not both.

•

Outside the mainstream press the news about Ukraine is a nonstop deluge of stories about how badly things are going for them.

Here are some recent articles from Antiwar.com:

"Ukraine's Top General Says Situation on the Battlefield Has 'Significantly Worsened'" discusses Ukrainian Commander-in-Chief Oleksandr Syrskyi's acknowledgement that Russia is making steady gains and that the frontlines in Ukraine are at risk of collapsing wherever Russia focuses its offensive.

"US General Says Russia's Military Is Bigger Than Before Ukraine Invasion" quotes General Christopher Cavoli saying "The army is actually now larger—by 15%—than it was when it invaded Ukraine," an acknowledgement that Washington's stated goal of using this proxy war to "weaken" Russia has failed.

"Russia Quickly Restores Oil Refinery Capability Hurt By Ukrainian Attacks" discusses how badly Russia is damaging Ukraine's energy infrastructure compared to the damage Ukraine has been able to deal to Russia's.

Here are a couple more from The Libertarian Institute:

"US Official Admits Ukraine Proxy War Failing to Weaken Russia" features an acknowledgement from Deputy Secretary of State Kurt Campbell that Russia has reconstituted nearly all of its military losses in Ukraine.

"Ukraine Tightens Rules on Military Service, Angering Soldiers" reports on how "Ukraine's legislature advanced multiple new laws that tighten rules on conscription and extend military services for those already in uniform."

It's absolutely criminal how the west pushed this country into sacrificing a generation to a war they always knew was unwinnable.

•

Caitlin Johnstone ✔
@caitoz

1. Deny bombing the consulate
2. Say the consulate wasn't really a consulate
3. Say Iran better not retaliate against you for that time you bombed the consulate
4. Say you had no idea that Iran would make such a big deal about you bombing their consulate

Left I on the News @leftiblog · 2h
Ri-i-i-ight. 🙄

Miscalculation Leads to Escalation as Israel and Iran Clash

Israeli officials say they didn't see a strike on an Iranian target in Syria as a provocation, and told the U.S. about it just moments before the attack.

11:37 AM · Apr 18, 2024 · **9,309** Views

144 Reposts   **4** Quotes   **371** Likes   **16** Bookmarks

•

So much suffering and loss has been caused by the way people decided a long time ago that killing one person is murder and therefore immoral but killing thousands of people is "war" and therefore fine. The actual act is the same; only the narrative and the scale are different.

•

Around the mid-1800s humanity began to notice it doesn't make sense for a small group of rich people to own everything and for everyone else to continually give that group labor, rent and expenses just to stay alive, and ever since then the media, the mainstream culture and the foreign policy of the ruling class have been intensely devoted to aggressively erasing this realization from humanity's memory.

Featured image via Adobe Stock.

Afshin Rattansi ✓
@afshinrattansi · Follow

X

"I want my legs back"

-11-year-old Palestinian girl Razan Muneer Arafat wakes
up to find her legs amputated, after she was injured by
US-UK-EU-armed Israeli airstrikes

Horror such as this, given the all clear by the US-led
'rules-based order'

rumble.com/v4ignal-gaza-w...

بدي رجلي ♥️

11 years old Palestinian girl Razan Muneer Arafat on crutches walks in a
makeshift tent in Rafah, Gaza on March 10, 2024. Razan lost her entire
family in an Israeli attack and was pulled from rubble alive yet has her
leg amputated. She is often seized by sudden crying jag due to her
trauma. She stays with her uncle's family who took refuge at a school in
Rafah, and dreams about having a prosthetic leg to continue her life on
her own, without depending on a wheelchair.

Jehad alshrafi

Watch on X

8:16 PM · Mar 15, 2024

♥ 220   💬 Reply   🔗 Copy link

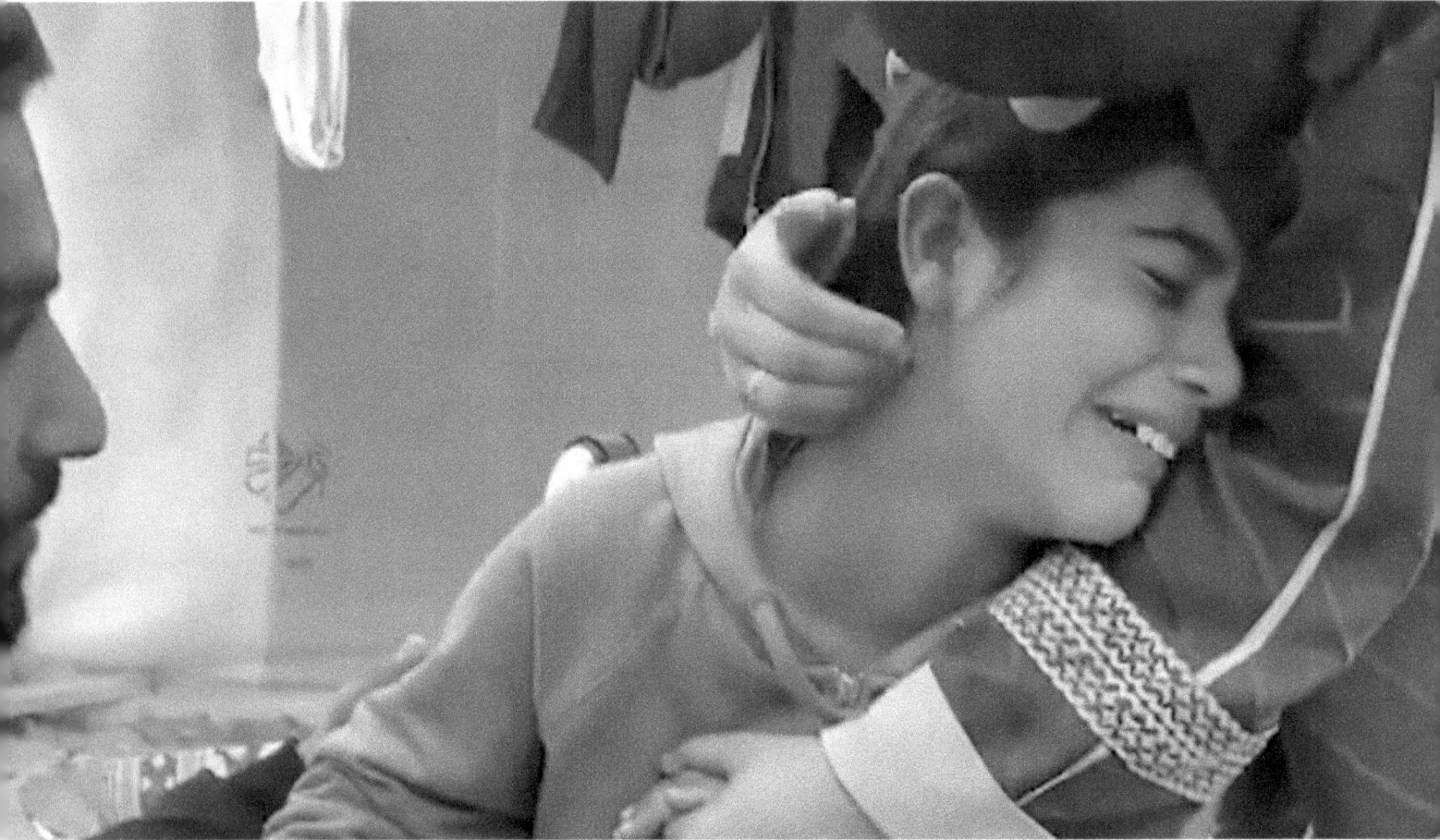

The Amputated Limbs Of Children

"I want my legs back," the girl cried in Arabic.
"I want my legs back."

You can't have your legs back, little girl.
They have been eaten by a hungry machine
who needs them for fuel to power its gears.

The machine needs your legs to keep the sky raining bombs
and to make its death robots fly.
Your legs power the bulldozers digging mass graves
and the tanks blowing holes in the hospitals.

A glorious kingdom is held together
by the amputated limbs of children.
A pentagon-shaped castle is built from the bones
of the amputated limbs of children.
Wall Street werewolves and bank boys dine
on the amputated limbs of children.
Movie stars treat their wrinkles with creams
made from the amputated limbs of children.
Suburban families prop up their smiles
with the amputated limbs of children.
The news man lies and in his eyes
you see the amputated limbs of children.
The podium man smirks and between his teeth
are the amputated limbs of children.

And the little girl cries,
and the news man ignores her,
and the podium man smirks at her,
and the bank boy bites her,
and the machine rolls on,
limbs fed into its furnace with pitchforks,
crushing houses and blackening the sky,
poisoning the oceans and bloodying the earth,
while the air fills with the crying of children,
for limbs that will never come back,
for homes that will never come back,
for mothers that will never come back,
for childhoods that will never come back,
for brightness that will never come back,
for innocence that will never come back,
for dreams that will never come back,
for joy that will never come back.

And we are here,
eating cheesy meatcarbs and watching funny haw-haws
and gossiping and prattling and wishing we looked better
and trying not to think about all the tiny arms and legs
we see covering the earth
whenever we step outside.

https://www.caitlinjohnst.one